Hanah and Kyle,

May your love forever grow!

With love from the Cranberry Creek team,

Leanna   Haylie

Kayleigh   Susan

Dylan

09/09/23 ♡

FEAD

/fēd/ (feed)

The act of giving food, to encourage growth, to satisfy.

———

Autumn Ongaro
Creator of Evolving Autumn

Editor: Julia Spiegl

ISBN: 978-1-7782134-0-3

In dedication to Maggie Mae

Contents

A Warm Welcome

―――――

This book will carry you through the four seasons in my kitchen using ingredients solely from the land of Norfolk County. At its heart, this is a story about eating: eating seasonally, locally and sustainably. I will share the stories of many farms and transform their ingredients into effortless dishes. Good food doesn't require extensive ingredient lists, complicated cooking techniques, or hard to find elements; good food simply showcases fresh, quality ingredients. The bounty of fresh foods found in Norfolk County were the inspiration for this book: allow FEAD to fuel your reconnection with how your food is grown and deepen the holistic relationship the land holds with your mind, body and soul.

This story begins about ten years ago when I wanted nothing more than to leave my home town in Norfolk County. I was graduating high school and was ready to experience the world without ever taking a look back at my small town. I spent years studying psychology, nutrition and education, travelling and heading down a career path that I eventually realized was not meant for me. Much to my dismay, I ended up back in Norfolk County. I felt entirely lost, disheartened and unsure of where my life was headed. I was able to find solace in the one thing that always brought me joy during difficult times by leaning into my creativity.

At that time, I felt the most at peace and free while experimenting in the kitchen. I wanted to share these experiments with others, so I began posting pictures taken on my cellphone of my dishes on Instagram. This quickly developed into studying how to properly style food and photograph it so that my pictures told a story. I continued working my nine-to-five job while dedicating my weekends to experimenting, failing and ultimately growing. Those weekends of cooking and photographing became the fire I was longing for.

In the spring of 2020, I officially started Evolving Autumn, my business focused on food photography and recipe development. Considering my business scope, I began sourcing more local ingredients, forming connections with local farmers and gaining a new appreciation for the county. Slowly, I started to feel admiration for all that Norfolk County encapsulates; the farms and the deep history they hold, the plethora of fresh ingredients, the wineries, the craft breweries and the passion for supporting the community. Norfolk County transformed into a special place for me as I realised why it is a special place for so many others.

Though I don't know where my journey is headed, I do know that creating this book by connecting with farmers, utilising ingredients at their prime and creating stories through my photography has brought such a spark that I was seeking all those years ago. I know that I am on the right path and I want to thank you for walking alongside me.

A Brief History of Agriculture in Norfolk County and an Ode to Tobacco

After some discussion with Historians and those who have studied small rural towns in Ontario, it was concluded that there is unfortunately not much cited and reliable information on Norfolk County. So, this brief history will be a collection of what has been cited, personal anecdotes and observance. Though there is a deep history far beyond what will be discussed, the focus will be on agriculture for the sake of this book.

The sand and silt that created the landform of this county were deposited from glacial lakes (meltwater of a glacier; Chapman and Putnam 251). Forests had grown slowly on the sand deposits of Norfolk County and as settlement began in the late 1700's, sawmills opened and attracted more workers and increased the population (TVO 16:13). The first European settlers were required by law to cut down trees to clear land for farming, so the forests were cleared and burned in order to retrieve ownership (TVO 16:20-16:34).

Unfortunately, this clearing caused open plains for windstorms causing precious topsoil loss and the light soil leftover could not hold up to regular cropping (TVO 16:44). The soil became exhausted and land productivity declined as the wind erosion continued, so families began to leave in search of fertile land (TVO 17:00; Chapman and Putnam 253). Now known as "Ontario's Garden" Norfolk County was once nearly a desert.

Due to the impoverished land, a furniture maker by the name of Walter McCall had to travel further and further for lumber. He refused to believe nothing could be done to save the land, so he planted a few saplings by his lumber mill as an experiment. McCall inspired Edmund Zavitz, a local forestry professor, and together they convinced the provincial government to purchase 100 acres of wasteland and open the St. Williams Forestry Station (now the St. Williams Nursery and Ecology Centre) in efforts to conserve the land. The county was home to its lowest population at the end of the first World War while the land remained idle in efforts of reforestation (TVO 17:30-18:13; Chapman and Putnam 253).

The Forestry Station team and volunteers planted around 350,000 pine and spruce seeds and several thousands of imported white pine seedlings. To their surprise, the trees rooted, grew and persevered through windstorms. As the trees matured, they collected the pine cones and developed a drying method to extract the seeds and produce more trees. The new seedlings were offered to farmers to plant to create hedgerows and woodlots to control wind and blowing sand, to help water infiltrate into the soil and to improve overall biodiversity. By the 1930's the Forestry Station had reforested thousands of acres of degraded land and was able to stabilize the soil with a monoculture of fast growing trees (TVO 18:34-19:30). Have you ever wondered why many of the older pine forests in Norfolk County are found growing in perfectly straight rows? This is why!

Around the same time as the reforestation efforts expanded, farmers discovered that the sandy soils of Norfolk were ideal for growing tobacco (TVO 21:00). The light soil provided easy tillage, ease of excavation and accessibility to water (Chapman and Putnam 255). The introduction of flue cured tobacco (a type of cigarette tobacco) drastically increased the value of tobacco crops and the high pay paired with the porous soil brought people back to the county and gave them an economic reason to stay (TVO 21:10-21:28). By 1931, around 16,000 acres of tobacco were being grown, naming Norfolk County the Ontario Tobacco Belt (Chapman and Putnam 253). Between the reforestation efforts and tobacco farming, the desert transformed into productive farmland with a prosperous agricultural industry (TVO 21:30-21:37). Tobacco growing took the leading role in farming and the curing kilns are now part of the landscape across the county.

Tobacco Kiln

Tobacco is still grown today, but with a few modern changes. It is propagated from seed in a greenhouse in late winter and then transplanted to the field in the late spring. Norfolk County offers an ideal growing environment as the plant grows optimally in sandy loam soil and at temperatures between 20 to 30°C. The sandy soil offers drainage, aeration, absorbs heat quickly in the day and cools off at night creating a moisturizing dew that helps the plants flourish.

The best quality tobacco leaves are produced when the flowerheads of the plants are removed. This process is known as topping and helps the plant's energy move away from the flowerhead to produce better quality tobacco leaves that mature more uniformly. Once the tobacco is ready for harvest, generally late July to early August, the leaves are removed from the stalk. Tobacco used to be tirelessly harvested by hand by bending over and picking the leaves one-by-one, thus giving it the name "the back-breaking leaf." Now the leaves are removed by a mechanized tobacco harvester in stages called a pass. Once harvested, the leaves are loaded onto racks and hung in curing kilns. Curing entails wilting, yellowing, colouring and drying. There are different forms of curing but for flue curing tobacco (as seen in the pictures on page 12), heat is applied to the tobacco leaves in ventilated kilns for around 9-10 days or until the desired chemical and physical changes are reached. Some say the best smell in the world is curing tobacco! The smell differs depending on the variety, but some describe it as smoky, sweet and earthy with hints of fresh cut grass, rose, black tea and vanilla. The cured tobacco is then transferred to the strip room where it is inspected, graded and bailed.

Tobacco farming holds a significant role in Norfolk County's agricultural history. Nearly every farm featured in this book was once a tobacco farm, but tobacco farming has come with its struggles. As health concerns around tobacco grew, the Ontario government stopped the tobacco quota system in 2008 offering the growers a federal buy-out package to stop their growing operations and to exit the dwindling industry. The farmers that agreed to the buy-out package are permitted to grow any crop except for tobacco and/or switch to raising livestock. The farmers who did not agree to the buy-out are still able to grow a regulated amount of tobacco but now require a special tobacco growing licence that was created in 2009. During the quota system, the price of tobacco was sanctioned by the government under the Ontario Flue-Cured Tobacco Grower's Marketing Board, but now it is up to the license holder to negotiate prices with the tobacco buyer.

To account for the loss of their tobacco crop, many farmers have diversified their crop selections to include fruit orchards, vegetables, ginseng and nuts as tobacco demand continues to decrease. However, these crops require much larger acreage and larger machinery to be profitable. To compromise for the additional acreage and sizeable machinery, hedgerows and other trees are starting to be removed once again. Are we headed back to a barren desert?

––––––––

If you would like to learn more about the history, heritage and culture of Norfolk County, please visit:

- Port Dover Harbour Museum

- The Waterford Heritage & Agricultural Museum

- Delhi Tobacco Museum and Heritage Centre

- Backus Mill Heritage and Conservation Centre

- Norfolk County Archives by Eva Brook Donly Museum

- Norfolk Arts Centre at Lynnwood National Historic Site

- Teeterville Pioneer Museum

Eating Seasonally and Locally

Each recipe in this book is based upon ingredients that grow seasonally within Norfolk County. The book is sectioned into the four seasons to encourage seasonal eating and the utilisation of ingredients at their peak flavour, texture and nutritional value.

As many produce items have become readily available at grocery stores all year round, a disconnect has unfortunately emerged between how our food grows, where it comes from and how it arrives on our plates. The grocery store is simple, organized and generally accessible. Though these are all great attributes, it provides us less room to be creative and curious with our food.

Eating seasonally and locally can start as small as you would like it to - it does not have to be a difficult or large change. It can be as simple as stopping at a roadside stand to buy a piece of fruit or walking through a farmer's market to simply see what's in season. It might feel overwhelming to go to a market with so many choices, colours and textures along with foods that have perhaps not been on display at the grocery store. Allow this discovery of new foods to be joyful! Let those colours and new textures guide you. What catches your eye? Is there an ingredient you had at a friend's house that you've been wanting to cook with? Maybe a nostalgic scent floats past you. Stay curious!

I have listed a few benefits of eating seasonally and locally below. I hope that they, along with the rest of the book, encourage you to liven up your dining table and enjoy the bounty of fresh foods just as nature intended.

It is Better For You. Food begins to lose nutrients as soon as it is harvested. Food travelling and sitting for less time will retain a greater flavour and nutrient value. It also honours your physiology as you feel the shifts of the seasons within you and notice your body naturally craving what the earth has to offer.

It Tastes Better. Eating seasonally allows the natural growing and ripening rhythms of the food to occur. When food is harvested out of its natural growing period, it must be artificially ripened, transported and exposed to extended chilling. These all change the texture, taste and nutritional value of the food. When fruits and vegetables have naturally ripened on the vine or tree they will offer much greater flavour and overall quality.

It Reduces Your Carbon Footprint. When food is shipped from afar, it must be packaged, transported and refrigerated. Buying locally and seasonally means less transportation, lower emissions from transportation vehicles and packaging facilities, less refrigeration and less food waste from damage during shipment.

It Builds Community. When you buy locally, you are supporting small businesses and families in your community and improving your local infrastructure. Maybe one week a tomato catches your eye at a market stall; you buy it, take it home, and are overjoyed with its flavour. The next week you return and ask the farmer how the tomato was grown and what makes it so delicious. You have now formed a connection and have a deeper understanding of how your food is grown.

This is what eating seasonally is all about; eating ingredients at their prime, supporting local and building community.

Before We Begin

Before we begin, please read over each recipe in full before making them. I have made each recipe approachable, yet with a fresh twist encouraging you to try something new. Because of this, some of the recipes require chilling, rising, long bake times etc. I would hate for you to start making something thirty minutes before dinner only to find out it needs two hours to chill- you know?

I have written many ingredient lists in both weight (grams and pounds) and volume (cups, tablespoons, teaspoons, etc.) measurements. It's okay if the volume measurements work better for you, but using a kitchen scale is a great way to add consistency to your kitchen adventures, especially for baked goods (like the meringues on page 106). A liquid measuring cup for ingredients listed in milliliters can be handy to have on hand too!

All of the recipes have been tested with the exact ingredients and ratios listed, so any substitutions may yield different results. I have listed a few ingredient recommendations below:

Salt. Nearly every recipe in this book uses salt. In my opinion, salt is the most important ingredient giving flavour to every dish, even desserts. There are many salt varieties to choose from, but I highly recommend kosher salt. Kosher salt is the least "salty" of the salts and has a wide, coarse grain which enhances the flavour of foods without overpowering. I especially recommend kosher salt over iodized table salt as the iodine can cause a bitter taste in foods. If you rather use the salt you have on hand, you may have to adjust the recipes to your liking (more or less salt). Start with less and add more if needed. Remember, salt equals flavour!

Butter. You will see that I only use unsalted butter throughout the book. This is more of a personal preference, but I find using unsalted butter gives me more control of how much salt is being added to a dish. If you prefer to use salted butter, you may have to reduce the amount of salt you add to the recipe.

Eggs. Eggs perform best in recipes when they are at room temperature. Room temperature eggs blend more evenly in batters, help dough rise and yield more volume. Cold eggs can result in lumpy texture, dense crumb and longer baking times. To quickly bring cold eggs to room temperature, place them in a bowl, fill with hot tap water and let them sit for 5-10 minutes.

As *FEAD* is based on the importance of local, fresh ingredients I recommend using these ingredients in the kitchen whenever possible!

I would LOVE to see the creations you make from this book. Share them on Instagram and tag me @evolvingautumn or on my Facebook page, Evolving Autumn.

SPR

ING

SPRING:

As the flowers awake, we hear a whisper of growth and rebirth. Feel the lightness and energy as we welcome back new blooms, sunshine and abundance.

As spring comes and new seeds are planted for harvest, take this time to also plant new seeds in your life. Seeds of purpose, adventure and change. Remember that seeds take time to grow and they must change to grow, but eventually they will flourish.

JLK Farms

asparagus

After a long winter, asparagus greets us with its bright green spears. It is a sure sign of spring when you spot "Asparagus" signs popping up on the side of the roads. This season is well known by first generation asparagus farmers Jake and Lisa Knelsen of JLK Farms.

The couple purchased a 50 acre farm in 2000, and have since grown their farming land to over 100 acres. They have rebuilt the farm from the ground up and take pride in growing food to feed their local community. A driving force for their commitment and hard work has been educating their children to value farming and fostering a connection to their food; farming instils the power of knowing where our food comes from and maintains the importance of dedication.

Asparagus plants require some planning and patience as they are slow to mature and will not be ready to harvest for at least

Jake and Lisa Knelsen with children Shawn and Julia

three years. These years allow the plant to fill-out and develop crowns (the root system of the asparagus plant). Once mature, the perennial will continue to produce for up to 15 years. The asparagus spears are all hand-picked and cut off just above the soil once they are around seven to ten inches tall. In Norfolk County, asparagus season is a quick two months, beginning in early May and ending in late June. Norfolk County grows more asparagus than any other region in Canada, making it Canada's top producer.

Roasted Asparagus Soup with Crispy Bacon

- Serves 4 -

Welcome spring with this rich, bright and velvety soup. The key to this soup is roasting the asparagus first to bring depth and pairing it with the bacon to help balance out the slightly-bitter flavour asparagus can have. This soup may just convert asparagus haters!

Ingredients

1 pound (455 g) fresh asparagus

1 tablespoon olive oil

6 slices bacon

2 garlic cloves, minced

2 cups (480 ml) chicken or vegetable stock

1 cup (240 ml) heavy cream

1/2 teaspoon + 1/4 teaspoon kosher salt

1/2 teaspoon ground black pepper

1 tablespoon lemon juice

Garnish

Fresh basil

Reserved asparagus and chopped bacon pieces

Directions

1. Preheat the oven to 425°F. Line a baking sheet with parchment paper.

2. Cut off and discard the lower third of the asparagus stalks (the hard, woody bottom). Place the asparagus onto the parchment lined baking sheet and toss with the oil and 1/2 teaspoon of salt. Arrange them in a single layer and roast for 12-15 minutes or until tender and browned.

3. In a large dutch oven, fry the bacon over medium heat until crispy, about 3-4 minutes each side. Let cool and then chop into 1/2 inch pieces.

4. Reserve 2 tablespoons of the bacon fat in the dutch oven (the rest can be discarded or reserved in the fridge to cook with later if desired). Heat over medium, add the garlic and sauté until fragrant, about 30 seconds.

5. Add in the asparagus and stir. Add in a 1/2 cup of the stock to deglaze the pot, scraping up any brown bits from the bottom.

6. Add the remaining stock to the pot and use an immersion blender to blend until smooth, about 1 minute. Alternatively, you can pour the soup into a high-speed blender and blend on high until smooth, about 1 minute, then pour back into the pot.

7. Heat over medium and once near a boil, stir in the chopped bacon pieces, heavy cream, remaining 1/4 teaspoon of salt and black pepper. Continue to stir until heated through, but do not allow it to boil. Stir in the lemon juice just before serving.

8. Spoon into serving bowls, top with the garnishes and serve. Store in an airtight container in the refrigerator for up to 3 days, or in the freezer for up to 1 month.

Meadow Lynn Farms

strawberries

Sharon and Fred Judd of Meadow Lynn Farms are well known in Norfolk County for their prize worthy strawberries. The farm was originally established with a humble 60 acres in 1946 as a dairy farm and they have continued to produce milk for the last 75 years. As generations were added, the farm has greatly evolved to a family farming affair of nearly 280 acres of strawberries, seasonal vegetables, grain crops and hay with baby Elizabeth marking the 5th generation at Meadow Lynn. Though the focus of this farm for

Sharon Judd with daughter-in-law Sarah Judd and baby Elizabeth

FEAD is the strawberries that grow on Meadow Lynn Farms, it would be a disservice to not mention that they also offer Community Supported Agriculture (or commonly known as CSA) boxes, grass-fed beef boxes and even seedlings for you to grow in your own garden!

The farm currently offers nine varieties of strawberries with varying levels of sweetness, firmness and size to provide you with the perfect product whether your strawberries will be used for jams, pies or a different culinary creation. Though one can find thousands of strawberry plants covering five and a half acres, Sharon continues to research and experiment finding new varieties to maintain the highest quality crop.

Strawberry plants are a perennial and cold-hardy, being able to survive our cold winters. They love lots of sun and moisture, and will naturally produce runners (daughter plants) that will root and grow into new plants, so they need plenty of space to spread and grow. Depending on the variety of the strawberry plant, harvest can last anywhere from three weeks to months, spanning from early June to late fall.

Mini Strawberry Cheesecake Hand Pies

- Makes 14 -

Strawberries are special as they are the first fruit to ripen in Ontario and often elicit nostalgic memories of sunshine, fresh air and stained shirts. I hope these hand pies bundle up those memories and bring back that happiness in every bite. They are a fun and mess-free option for gatherings or as a quick snack.

Ingredients

Dough

1/2 cup (113 g) unsalted butter, at room temperature

1/2 cup (113 g) cream cheese, at room temperature

3/4 cup (94 g) all-purpose flour, plus more for dusting

1/2 cup (55 g) graham crumbs

1/2 teaspoon kosher salt

1 egg, beaten

Filling

2 tablespoons (16 g) cornstarch, sifted

2 tablespoons (25 g) brown sugar

1 cup finely chopped strawberries (about 10 regular strawberries)

1/4 cup (57 g) cream cheese, chopped into small cubes

1 tablespoon maple syrup

2 teaspoons lemon zest

1/2 teaspoon vanilla

Pinch of kosher salt

Glaze

1/2 cup (65 g) icing sugar, sifted

1-2 tablespoons milk

Directions

1. **To prepare the dough**, use a stand mixer fitted with the paddle attachment to cream the butter and cream cheese together until smooth and fluffy.

2. Add in the flour, graham crumbs and salt. Mix until just combined.

3. Transfer the dough onto a lightly floured surface. Gently knead for about one minute and then shape into a ball and wrap with plastic wrap. Refrigerate for at least one hour.

4. **To prepare the filling**, whisk the cornstarch and brown sugar together in a medium bowl. Add in the strawberries and cream cheese and toss to coat. Stir in the maple syrup, lemon zest, vanilla and salt.

5. Preheat the oven to 350°F. Line a baking sheet with parchment paper. Remove the dough from the refrigerator 10 minutes before you're ready to use it.

6. Unwrap the dough, place it between 2 sheets of parchment paper and roll it to about an 1/8 inch thickness.

7. Use a 3-inch round cookie cutter to cut the dough into circles. Form the remaining dough back into a ball, roll out again and cut out more circle. Repeat this step until you have 14 circles.

8. Stir the filling and add about one heaping tablespoon to the middle of each circle. Fold over into a half moon shape and use a fork to crimp the edges together and to poke a couple steam holes in the top of each pie.

9. Place the pies onto the parchment lined baking sheet and brush with the beaten egg. Bake for 25-30 minutes or until golden brown. Remove from the oven and let cool for 5 minutes.

10. **To prepare the glaze**, whisk the icing sugar and milk together until smooth. Start with one tablespoon of milk and add more until desired consistency is reached. Drizzle the glaze over the pies and serve. Store in an airtight container in the refrigerator for up to 3 days.

Freezer Friendly. Follow steps 1-9 and store in an airtight container lined with parchment paper for up to 1 month. Microwave for 30-45 seconds or reheat in the oven at 400°F for 15-20 minutes, or until warmed through. Prepare glaze, drizzle on and serve.

Lovell Springs

Rainbow Trout

Beginning in 2007, Sean of Lovell Springs has made it his passion to create a sustainable and ethical Rainbow Trout fishery. Lovell Springs is distinct from most fisheries as the trout are raised in fresh spring water flowing through the forest and below the forest floor, collecting many nutrient-rich micro-organisms along the way. The continuous flow of fresh spring water makes it possible to rear healthy fish without the use of hormones, steroids, antibiotics or chemicals. The spring flows into cement raceways which hold the fish and provide plenty of room to eat, swim and spawn. As they are spring water fed, up to a third of their diet is natural aquatic and terrestrial insects (with the rest being supplemented with pellets).

A sign that the water quality is high is the inhabitation of the Caddisfly as the oxygen content in the water is important to their survival. The larvae form protection by webbing together a hollow case made from debris including sticks, rocks and leaves found in the water (as seen on page 29). This acts as a cocoon until they are mature enough to crawl to the water surface. Caddisflies are also one of the natural food sources for the Rainbow Trout.

Additionally, the trout eat beach hoppers (also known as fairy shrimp), an ant-size crustacean that munches on microalgaes and yeasts within the water. These freshwater algaes and yeasts naturally create a red pigment called astaxanthin. The flowing spring transports the beach hoppers which are eaten by the trout who accumulate the astaxanthin in their muscle, skin and eggs creating the beautiful shades of pink, purple, red and orange.

Sean of Lovell Springs and Jess of Matz Fruit Barn are partners both in life and in farming. The trout farm contributes greatly to the sustainability measures found at Matz Fruit Barn (please see page 64) by utilizing the nutrient-rich remainders of the trout farm that would otherwise be discarded including fish fertilizer, hydrolysate and dried algae. Each week the fish detritus (waste, dead matter and fecal material) is vacuumed out and is used to support plants when being transplanted out into the field and throughout the season, almost like a fish-based manure. Another form of fertilizer used is the fish hydrolysate where the bones and scraps of the fish are fermented down into a nutrient-rich liquid filled with essential amino acids, vitamins, minerals, oils and enzymes. Not only does this process allow for all parts of the fish to be used, but it also provides the earth with the many nutrients it needs to produce quality produce.

Furthermore, the algae from the spring water that the trout reside in is collected and dried in the sun and then sprinkled in the soil and around the plants to provide nutrients, but more profoundly, to offer frost protection! The algae themselves produce a kind of antifreeze which keeps their bodies liquid even when temperatures fall below zero degrees. When fed to plants, it increases the plant's stress tolerance and offers protection from the frost. Also, a protein in algae called florigen induces flowering in plants and helps produce healthy blossoms. How amazing!

The trout are truly a labour of love as everything is done by hand including the feeding, catching and processing. They take around three years to mature and once processed, the fish are never frozen and delivered within 24 hours of harvest. You can purchase Lovell Springs Rainbow Trout filleted, dressed or smoked at Matz Fruit Barn. You can also find Lovell Springs and Matz Fruit Barn at Trinity Bellwoods Farmers Market in Toronto on Tuesdays.

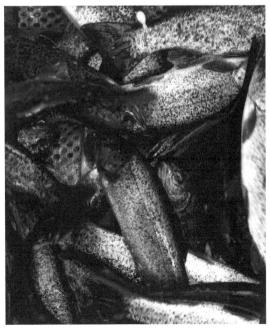

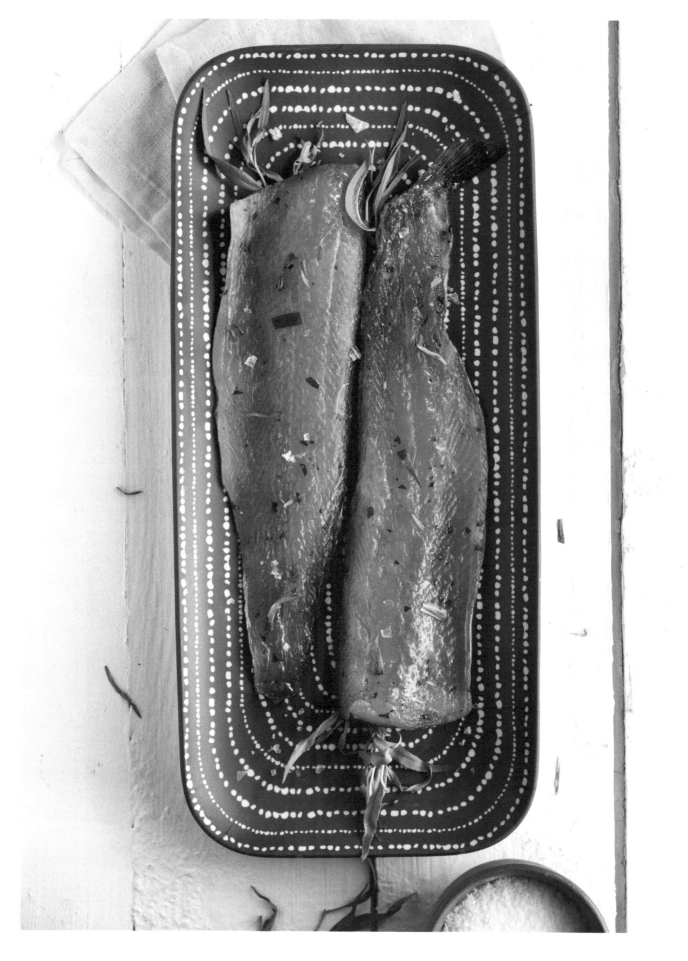

Coriander and Caraway Rainbow Trout Gravlax

- Serves 4 -

This recipe was inspired by my Au Pair experience in Sweden. Salmon gravlax was a regular part of gathering boards and breakfast plates. Though fish for breakfast may not sound appealing to you, this Scandinavian-style cold-cured Rainbow Trout is sure to wow guests with its colourful flavour and silky, raw-like texture. Enjoy it on charcuterie boards, with pumpernickel bread and onions or add major flavour to your next salad.

Ingredients

2 Rainbow Trout fillets, around 300 g (must be fresh)

1/2 cup (100 g) kosher salt

1/2 cup (100 g) granulated sugar

1 tablespoon lemon zest

1/2 heaping teaspoon caraway seeds

1/2 teaspoon ground black pepper

1/2 cup fresh coriander (cilantro), chopped

1/4 cup fresh tarragon, chopped

Directions

1. Line a baking dish with enough plastic wrap to fully cover the fillets. The dish should be wide enough to hold both fillets flat and deep enough to hold some liquid that will be released as the trout cures.

2. Add the salt, sugar, lemon zest, caraway and pepper to a food processor. Pulse until combined.

3. Evenly spread half of the salt and sugar mixture into your dish and then cover with half of the chopped coriander and half of the chopped tarragon.

4. Place the trout fillets in the dish skin-side down.

5. Cover the fillets with the remaining coriander and tarragon and then the remaining salt and sugar mixture ensuring the fillets are completely covered.

6. Fold the plastic wrap over to form a package with all the contents inside.

7. Leave to macerate in the refrigerator for 24 hours.

8. Rinse with cold water and pat dry with an absorpent towel. Cut into slices and serve. Store in an airtight container in the refrigerator for up to 3 days.

Rhubarb Custard Pie

- Serves 8 -

In the springtime, the pink and green ombre stalks of rhubarb begin to emerge from the ground. Although technically a vegetable, the stalks of rhubarb are generally treated like a fruit. When raw, rhubarb is very sour! (If you have ever bitten into raw rhubarb, you know just what I mean.) However, this tartness brings the perfect balance to this sweet and creamy custard pie.

When picking or buying rhubarb, look for plump, firm stalks with red throughout. Generally stalks with more red are younger, sweeter and more tender, while more green stalks are older and less flavourful.

Ingredients

Pie Crust

1 9-inch frozen pie crust in a pie plate or the fresh galette dough from page 67

Filling

3 cups (around 360 g) + 2 cups (around 240 g) raw rhubarb, chopped

1/2 cup (100 g) + 1 cup (200 g) granulated sugar

3 tablespoons (24 g) all-purpose flour

1/4 teaspoon cardamom

1/4 teaspoon nutmeg

Pinch of kosher salt

2 large eggs, at room temperature

2 tablespoons heavy cream, at room temperature

1/2 teaspoon vanilla extract

To Serve

Whipped cream

Directions

1. Prepare pie crust according to the instructions. Frozen pie crusts may need pre-baking.

2. If using the galette dough recipe from page 67, follow steps 2-4. Remove from the fridge. On a lightly floured work surface, or between two sheets of parchment paper, roll the dough into a circle about 12 inches in diameter. Transfer the dough to a 9-inch pie plate. Gently fit the dough to the pie plate, trim any excess dough and crimp the edge as desired. Prick the bottom of the pie dough with a fork to prevent bubbling.

3. Preheat the oven to 400°F.

4. In a large saucepan over medium heat, add the 3 cups of rhubarb and the 1/2 cup of sugar and stir. Cook for 8-10 minutes or until the rhubarb is softened and any released water has reduced (you do not want this to be watery).

5. In a large bowl, combine the remaining 1 cup of sugar, flour, cardamom, nutmeg and salt.

6. In a separate bowl, whisk the eggs, cream and vanilla together until thickened and light in colour. Pour into the dry ingredients and stir until smooth and combined. Fold in the cooked rhubarb.

7. Pour into the prepared pie crust. Place the additional rhubarb pieces on top. I designed mine into a herringbone pattern with alternate rows of red and green rhubarb pieces (as seen on the previous page), but design yours however you would like!

8. Bake for 45-55 minutes or until set in the middle. Remove and let the pie cool completely before slicing. Enjoy with whipped cream. Store in the refrigerator for up to 2 days.

Roasted Radishes with Fresh Dill Cream

- Serves 4 -

If you have never tried roasted radishes, please try them as soon as possible! Roasting radishes takes away the sting and turns them sweet and almost potato-like. I love leaving the root tail on each end as they get extra crispy in the oven and add another layer of texture.

When preparing your radishes, save the greens! These greens are edible and make a great addition to salads, soups or simply sautéed with a little butter and garlic. Just make sure you give them a good wash as they tend to hold a lot of sand.

Ingredients

Radishes

1 pound radishes (around 20 radishes)

1 tablespoon olive oil

1/2 teaspoon kosher salt

1/2 teaspoon ground black pepper

1 tablespoon lemon juice

Fresh Dill Cream

1/2 cup (120 ml) heavy cream

1/4 cup dill, packed

1 teaspoon grainy mustard

1 teaspoon maple syrup

1/2 teaspoon kosher salt

1/2 teaspoon ground black pepper

Directions

1. Preheat the oven to 425ºF. Line a baking sheet with parchment paper.

2. Thoroughly wash radishes, remove the greens and cut in half lengthwise. Place onto the parchment lined baking sheet and toss them with the oil, salt and pepper. Spread them out and roast for 25-30 minutes or until tender and browned.

3. For the dill cream, add all ingredients to a high-speed blender and blend on high for 15 seconds or until slightly thickened and combined; this will not take long. If you accidentally over-blend and it becomes too thick, slowly blend in a little water 1 teaspoon at a time until desired consistency is reach. It should be thickened but still easy to pour.

4. Toss the radishes with the lemon juice, drizzle on the dill cream and serve.

Farmhouse Omelette

- Serves 2 -

I couldn't complete this book without giving an homage to the versatile egg. Eggs represent new life and rebirth and mark the arrival of spring, with (some) hens returning to egg laying in the spring after allowing their bodies to rest over the winter.

Eggs make a delicious and nutritious breakfast and add structure, richness, flavour and colour to many recipes. Thank you chickens!

Ingredients

4 slices thick-cut bacon

2 tablespoons unsalted butter

1/4 cup sweet onion, finely chopped

1/2 cup small-diced new potatoes

4 large eggs, at room temperature

2 tablespoons heavy cream

1/4 teaspoon kosher salt

1/4 teaspoon ground black pepper

1/8 teaspoon smoked paprika

2 tablespoons thinly sliced green onion, divided

1/2 cup grated old cheddar cheese

Directions

1. In a large skillet, cook the bacon over medium heat until crispy, around 3-4 minutes each side. Remove and place on a plate lined with paper towels to cool. Chop into 1/2 inch pieces.

2. Drain bacon grease from the skillet and melt the butter over medium-high heat. Add the onion and potato, and sauté until the potatoes are browned and tender, around 8-10 minutes.

3. In a medium bowl, whisk the eggs and cream until incorporated. Whisk in the salt, pepper and smoked paprika. Pour over the potatoes and onions. Sprinkle with the chopped bacon and 1 tablespoon of the green onions. Let cook for 4-5 minutes or until the eggs are set.

4. Sprinkle with the grated cheddar cheese and use a spatula to gently fold the omelette in half and cook for an additional 1-2 minutes.

5. Sprinkle with the remaining 1 tablespoon of green onions and serve immediately.

left to right: goose egg, duck egg, chicken egg

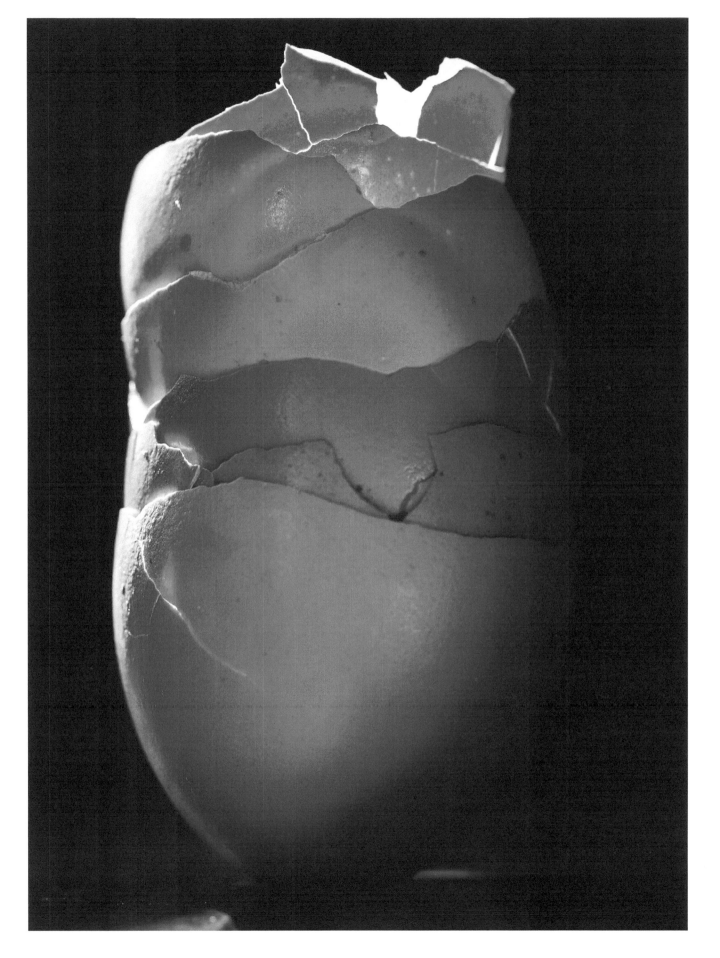

SUM

MER

SUMMER:

Welcome the increasing energy,
early mornings, the sweetest fruit
you have ever tasted and late
nights with sunsets more beautiful
than the last.

The seeds you planted in the
spring, both in life and for harvest,
are now reaching full bloom.
Harness the nourishment that is
needed to grow and evolve.

Move throughout your day
emulating the patterns of the sun;
spread light, nurture others and
honour the light within.

Schuyler Farms LTD

tart cherries

Family owned and operated Schuyler Farms LTD specializes in apples, grains and tart cherries. They also manage the Norfolk Cherry Company that was established in 1974 after a local processor shut down abruptly. The cherry farmers in the region had to decide if they were going to pull out their trees or put up their own processing plant. A group of producers banded together and set up a cooperative: The Norfolk Cherry Company. They now handle 80-90% of the tart cherries in all of Ontario and are one of the few cherry operations left in Canada for several reasons; cherries are a long-term crop that require a great deal of time and commitment, with little profit in the first many years; cherry harvest requires specialised equipment and the processing facility must be in close proximity as the time-sensitive cherries must be chilled and processed promptly after harvest; and most cherry farmers have retired and not many young people have the capital to invest, or the incentive as cherry prices have historically been quite low.

Cherries are mechanically harvested using a specific machine known as a hydraulic tree shaker (as seen in the images on page 47). A hydraulic arm clasps around the tree trunk, while a second machine wraps a tarp around the base of the tree at the same time. Using the hydraulic arm as the control, the machine vibrates to release the cherries from the tree onto the tarp below. The machine is calibrated to provide just enough vibration to shake off the cherries without damaging the tree. The cherries are then transferred to a large storage container filled with chilled water which firms the cherries and makes them more resilient for further processing. The growing, picking, sorting, pitting, and packaging of the cherries all happen in Norfolk County before being distributed widely to be used in bakery products or juice.

Cherry season is very short, as the entire harvest period only lasts for two to three weeks per year. The magnitude of the labour that goes into these weeks is apparent when we consider that up to 12 million pounds of cherries are packed and shipped per season! The short season in combination with this being one of the few cherry operations left in Canada, means swift action must be taken when hurdles arise such as a tree shaker part breaking or a processing machine requiring maintenance. This sometimes results in driving all the way to Michigan (the closest supplier and the cherry capital of the world) and back without a break to retrieve a machine part.

The unpredictable spring weather of Norfolk County can also serve as a problem: If the tree has blossomed and the temperature drops below zero degrees celsius, there's a risk of losing the whole crop as the frost will kill the blossoms. Luckily there are frost fans that can be used to blow air through the trees to prevent frost in those situations. It is due to the collective effort, innovation and dedication of many people that this operation continues today.

Tart Cherry Crumble Bars

- Serves 6 -

Cherries remind me of the summer days when I would go grocery shopping with my mom and we would eat an entire bag of cherries on the car ride home. There was no stopping us!

These bars are reminiscent of a cherry pie, but better in my opinion. I'm a huge fan of anything with a crumble topping, especially when paired with the adventurous flavour of tart cherries. This dessert can also be enjoyed straight out of the oven as a fruit crisp if bars aren't really your thing.

Ingredients

Crumble

2 cups (160 g) rolled oats

2 cups (250 g) all-purpose flour

3/4 cup (150 g) brown sugar, lightly packed

1/2 cup (100 g) granulated sugar

1/2 teaspoon baking soda

1/2 teaspoon cardamom

1/2 teaspoon kosher salt

3/4 cup (170 g) melted unsalted butter

1/3 cup (80 ml) maple syrup

Filling

Scant 2 1/2 cups (425 g) fresh or frozen pitted tart cherries

1/4-1/2 cup (50-100 g) white granulated sugar (depending on desired sweetness)

3 tablespoons (23 g) cornstarch

1 tablespoon lemon zest

1 tablespoon lemon juice

Directions

1. If the cherries are frozen, place them in a colander and run warm water over them to separate and let them drain for one hour. Discard juice.

2. Preheat the oven to 350°F. Line a 8 x 12-inch pan with parchment paper.

3. **To prepare the crumble**, whisk the oats, flour, brown sugar, granulated sugar, baking soda, cardamom and salt together in a large bowl. Ensure there are no clumps of brown sugar. Pour in the melted butter and the maple syrup and mix until you get a crumble-like texture.

4. Press 2/3 of the crumble into the parchment lined pan and bake for 10 minutes.

5. **To prepare the filling**, add all filling ingredients to a large bowl and mix until evenly combined and the cherries are coated. I like the bars more tart and use a 1/4 cup of sugar, but you can add up to a 1/2 cup of sugar for a sweeter bar.

6. Evenly spread the filling over the crumble bottom. Sprinkle on the remaining crumble and bake for 25-30 minutes, or until golden brown.

7. Remove from the oven and let sit to cool for at least one hour. The longer they sit, the more set and chewy they will become. Store in an airtight container at room temperature for up to 3 days.

Blueberry Hill Estates

blueberries

The story of Blueberry Hill Estates begins in 2005 when the Vranckx family purchased the farm. Established by the agricultural knowledge of the Weber and Dreiger families before them, the Vranckx family has managed to keep the nearly 50-year-old blueberry patch thriving, expanding it to include 13 different varieties across 15 acres.

On average, blueberry plants have a 25-year lifespan which makes this the oldest high-bush blueberry patch in Ontario. Norfolk's acidic soil is partially to thank for this as the soil naturally carries required minerals needed to nourish the blueberry bush through its root system. With proper care, the blueberry bushes will bear fruit from early July to the end of August.

The farm is proudly family-owned and operated and offers freshly picked blueberries in-store as well as a pick-your-own system which encourages their customers to harvest and form a deepend connection to the fruit that they will be taking home. The Vranckx family has also utilised the many fresh flavours of Norfolk County such as strawberries, raspberries, beets and peppers into the production of Front Road Market preserves and have developed their own winery and cidery, Front Road Cellars.

Blueberry Pop Tarts with Brown Butter Basil Icing

- Makes 4 -

These are a fun twist on a childhood classic! The flaky tart crust is filled with plump blueberries and smothered in an alluring basil icing. The fresh basil tames the tartness of the blueberries and gives the pastry complexity.

Ingredients

Dough

1 1/2 cups (188 g) all-purpose flour

1/2 teaspoon kosher salt

10 tablespoons (142 g) cold unsalted butter chopped into small cubes

1-3 tablespoons cold water

1 egg, beaten

Filling

1 overflowing cup fresh blueberries

1/3 cup (70 g) brown sugar, lightly packed

1 tablespoon (14 g) melted unsalted butter

1 tablespoon (8 g) cornstarch

2 large basil leaves, finely chopped

Icing

1/3 cup (76 g) unsalted butter

4 large basil leaves

1/2 cup (113 g) cream cheese at room temperature

1/2 cup (65 g) icing sugar

1/2 teaspoon lemon zest

1/2 teaspoon vanilla extract

1 tablespoon heavy cream

Directions

1. **To prepare the dough**, place the flour and salt in a food processor and pulse a few times to mix. Add in the cold butter cubes and pulse around 10 times or until the butter is in small clumps. Turn on the food processor and add in the water one tablespoon at a time until the dough comes together and forms a ball.

2. Transfer the dough onto a lightly floured surface. Gently knead for about one minute, shape into a ball and wrap with plastic wrap. Refrigerate for at least one hour.

3. **To prepare the filling**, add the blueberries to a medium bowl and use a fork to gently squish about half of them. Add the rest of the filling ingredients and stir to combine and coat the blueberries.

4. Preheat the oven to 425°F. Line a baking sheet with parchment paper. Remove the dough from the fridge 10 minutes before you're ready to use it.

5. Lightly flour the working surface and rolling pin. Split the dough into 4 equal pieces. Roll each piece into a thin rectangle, about an 1/8 inch thick. Use a knife or pizza wheel to cut out two equal sized rectangles. Repeat this step with the remaining dough until you have 8 rectangles, roughly equal in size.

6. Stir the filling and equally divide it between 4 of the rectangles, around a 1/4 cup of filling for each. Keep the filling a 1/4 inch away from the edge. Lay the other rectangles on top, lining up the edges and use a fork to crimp the edges and to poke a couple steam holes on the top of each tart.

7. Carefully transfer the tarts to the baking sheet and brush with the beaten egg. Bake for 25-30 minutes or until golden brown and bubbling. Remove from the oven and let cool.

8. **To prepare the icing**, place the butter and basil leaves in a medium-sized pan over medium heat. Once melted, the butter will begin to foam and sizzle. Occasionally stir to make sure the butter does not burn. After 5-8 minutes, the foam will subside and the butter will turn golden brown and smell nutty and sweet. Remove from the heat and transfer to a bowl. Place the bowl in the freezer for 10-20 minutes or until it has firmed back up to *room temperature* butter.

9. In a stand mixer fitted with the paddle attachment, cream the browned butter (with the basil leaves) and cream cheese until smooth and fluffy, about 3 minutes. Add in the icing sugar in two additions, mixing after each. Add in the lemon zest, vanilla and heavy cream and whip for 2 minutes on medium-high or until light and fluffy. Spread the icing onto the tarts and serve.

Freezer Friendly. Follow steps 1-7 and store in an airtight container lined with parchment paper for up to 1 month. Microwave for 45-60 seconds or reheat in the oven at 400°F for 15-20 minutes, or until warmed through. Prepare the icing, spread on and serve.

Gunther's Sweet Corn

sweet corn

Gunther's Sweet Corn is a multi-generational farm that has been operating since 1991. Like many farms in Norfolk County, their main crop started as tobacco. In 2007, they transitioned into other crops, including asparagus, ginseng and squash.

You can feel the connection fourth generation farmer Tom has to the farm as he explains his fond memories of riding in tractors with his dad, working the dirt and establishing that deep relationship with the land. Tom and his partner Alicia are proud of keeping the farm on a smaller scale to continue setting an example of interconnection. Gunther's Sweet Corn is extra special because every cob of corn is hand harvested by Tom's mother Helga. Each year, Helga carefully chooses corn varieties, coordinates planting and picks the corn - rain or shine - to ensure the freshest product each day.

Sweet corn comes in many varieties with varying levels of sweetness and has a fairly long growing period of 60 to 100 days. The plant likes warm soil and has shallow roots, so it needs to be well watered. The ovules of the plant will develop into kernels of corn once the silk (female) is pollinated by the tassel (male) with the help of the wind. Every strand of silk is connected to a corn ovule, which is why corn shucking can be tedious at times - all those straggly bits are actually the silk strongly attached to each of the kernels! It is truly amazing how intricately connected the plant is. Sweet corn is ready for harvest when the silk tops are brown, and the kernels are milky when pierced, around mid to late July until early September.

Roasted Sweet Corn and Leek Bisque

- Serves 4 -

A simple celebration of one of summer's most cherished gifts: sweet corn. A delicate harmony is formed between the subtle sharpness of the leeks and the familiar sweetness of the corn. Try this bisque hot or cold as an appetizer or as an accompaniment to your favourite seasonal meal. It pairs wonderfully with the Green Onion and Cheddar Dinner Rolls on page 63.

Ingredients

3 cups sweet corn kernels (around 4-6 ears of corn)

1 tablespoon olive oil

1/2 teaspoon + 1 teaspoon kosher salt

2 tablespoons (28 g) unsalted butter

1 cup thinly sliced leeks

1 large carrot, chopped into small cubes (about 1 cup)

2 garlic cloves, minced

1 tablespoon finely chopped sage, plus more for garnish

4 cups (960 ml) chicken or vegetable stock

1 cup (240 ml) heavy cream

1 teaspoon ground black pepper

1/4 teaspoon smoked paprika

1/8 teaspoon cayenne pepper (optional)

Directions

1. Preheat the oven to 450°F. Line a baking sheet with parchment paper.

2. Spread the corn kernels onto the baking sheet and toss with the oil and 1/2 teaspoon of salt. Roast for 20-25 minutes or until golden.

3. Melt the butter over medium heat in a large pot. Add the leeks and sauté until golden, about 5 minutes.

4. Add in the carrot, garlic, sage and roasted corn. Reserve a small amount of the corn for garnish if you would like. Sauté until fragrant, about 30 seconds.

5. Add in about a 1/4 cup of the stock to deglaze the pot first, scraping up any brown bits, then add in the rest. Cover with a lid and simmer for around 10 minutes or until the carrots are tender and cooked through.

6. Remove from the heat and use an immersion blender to blend until smooth, about 1 minute. Alternatively, you can pour the soup into a high speed blender and blend on high until smooth, about 1 minute, then pour back into the pot.

7. Stir in the heavy cream, pepper, smoked paprika, cayenne, and remaining 1 teaspoon of salt and heat on low until heated through. If serving cold, chill the soup in the fridge for at least 8 hours or overnight. If the soup is too thick, add in more stock or water until desired consistency is reached. Distribute among serving bowls, top with any reserved roasted corn and the extra sage and serve. Store in an airtight container in the refrigerator for up to 3 days, or in the freezer for up to 1 month.

Ryder Farms

green onions

The Ryder family has been farming the sandy soils of Norfolk County for over 100 years. Jason and Jackie Ryder took over the farm in 2003 and have continued to expand the farm, explore alternative crops and take on new sustainability measures. Originally producers of tobacco and winter vegetables, their main commodities are now green onions, asparagus, ginseng, sweet potatoes and grains.

Today, Ryder Farms grows approximately 120 acres of green onions, yielding around one million onions per acre. This makes Ryder Farms the largest, solely-owned green onion producer in Ontario, with their harvest season running from the beginning of July to the end of October. Green onions are densely planted as an annual crop and are harvested by hand by pulling the onions up by their shallow roots and bunching them with rubber bands right in the field. They are then quickly transported to be cleaned, graded and cooled.

Quick Green Onion and Cheddar Dinner Rolls

- Makes 12 -

These delicate dinner rolls are loaded with flavourful green onions and cheddar. They require just one hour of rising time and make a great addition to any meal.

Ingredients

- 3/4 cup (180 ml) warm whole milk (around 110°F)
- 1/4 cup (57 g) unsalted butter, melted and cooled
- 2 large eggs, at room temperature
- 1 teaspoon instant dry yeast
- 2 tablespoons granulated sugar
- 1 1/2 teaspoons + 1/2 teaspoon kosher salt
- 2 1/2 cups (315 g) all-purpose flour
- 1/2 cup finely chopped green onions
- 1/2 cup grated cheddar cheese

Directions

1. Line a baking sheet with parchment paper.

2. Combine the milk, butter, one egg, yeast, sugar and 1 1/2 teaspoons of salt in a large bowl. Add the flour and mix until just combined then gently fold in the green onions and cheddar cheese.

3. Transfer the dough to an oiled surface (I prefer to lay out parchment paper and drizzle it with oil rather than directly on the counter top) and knead until the dough is smooth and not sticky. Knead by pushing the dough down and outward and then fold in half towards you and repeat. The dough is ready when you can gently push your finger in and it bounces right back. If an indent stays, keep kneading. This may take up to 5 minutes.

4. Divide the dough into 12 equal pieces and shape each piece into a smooth ball. Place on the baking sheet, cover with plastic wrap or a damp cloth and let rise in a warm spot for one hour or until doubled in size. If you don't have a warm spot in your house, set the rolls in the oven with the light on.

5. Preheat the oven to 375°F (remove the rolls first if they were rising in the oven).

6. Beat the remaining egg and brush it on the buns and sprinkle on the remaining 1/2 teaspoon of salt. Bake for 20 minutes or until golden. Let cool before serving. Store in an airtight container at room temperature for up to 2 days.

Matz Fruit Barn

peaches

Matz Fruit Barn, located just outside of Port Dover, has been operating since 1962. Their mission is to share quality produce while ensuring the continued respect of the land it cultivates. They are proud stewards of the land and utilize sustainable and organic farming practices for a healthy microbial life within the soil. Part of the sustainability measures found at Matz are strongly correlated to utilizing nutrient-rich remainders of Lovell Springs trout farm that would otherwise be discarded including fish fertilizer, hydrolysate and dried algae (please see preceding page 29 for a detailed explanation). Thanks to these practices, you will find quality produce all season long at Matz Fruit Barn including peaches, melons, tomatoes, squash, apples, corn, potatoes and more. They also participate in Community Supported Agriculture (CSA) to share their bounty and to connect the community with their local farmers.

Norfolk County is a favourable growing area for peaches as peach trees prefer soil that is well drained and slightly acidic. Peaches are harvested completely by hand into eleven quart baskets which hold two layers of peaches. Once the baskets are full they are transferred into the barn to fulfil the day's order and the rest are transferred to the cooler for later sales.

Contrary to popular belief, peaches do not ripen as they sit. Matz Fruit Barn ensures the peaches are given the time to naturally develop sweetness and flavour on the tree, and are not picked before they are ready. A benefit of doing everything by hand is that it allows for the handling of more fragile produce. The cell development of a ripe peach is so full that when pressure is applied, the cells easily rupture which causes bruising, spoilage and ultimately decay. Handling these precious peaches would not be possible in a large-scale farming and shipping environment. A firm green peach on the other hand does not have the same cell development and is much more hearty to handle; but this comes at the cost of flavour and nutritional value. This is why imported peaches are nowhere near as delicious as fresh, Norfolk County peaches! Peaches are available at Matz Fruit Barn late July into late August.

Grilled Peach Galette

- Serves 8 -

The magical flavour of sweet, juicy and smoky grilled peaches are the star of this stunning dessert. Bake it in the oven or complete the entire cooking process on your grill to bring a surprising char to your comforting pie crust.

Ingredients

Dough

1 1/2 cups (188 g) all-purpose flour

1/2 teaspoon kosher salt

10 tablespoons (142 g) cold unsalted butter chopped into small cubes

2-3 tablespoons cold water

1 egg, beaten

Turbinado or raw sugar (optional)

Filling

10 ripe peaches

2 tablespoons + 2 tablespoons melted unsalted butter

1/2 cup (110 g) brown sugar, packed

2 tablespoons (16 g) cornstarch

1 tablespoon lemon juice

Pinch of kosher salt

Fresh basil (optional)

Directions

1. **To prepare the dough**, place the flour and salt in a food processor and pulse a few times to mix. Add in the cold butter cubes and pulse around 10 times or until the butter is in small clumps. Turn on the food processor and add in the water one tablespoon at a time until the dough comes together and forms a ball.

2. Transfer dough onto a lightly floured surface. Gently knead for about one minute, shape into a ball and wrap with plastic wrap. Refrigerate for at least 1 hour.

3. **Prepare the heat source**. The peaches can be grilled over hot coals of an open fire (wait until the smoke has calmed) or on a barbeque at medium-high heat.

4. **To prepare the filling**, cut the peaches in half and remove the pits. Brush with 2 tablespoons of melted butter and place them cut-side down and grill for 5 minutes, or until charred and softened. Remove from the heat and let cool enough to handle, about 10 minutes.

5. Remove the skin from the peaches (it should easily peel off if they are cooked enough) and slice each of the halves into thirds. Place the peach slices into a medium bowl with any liquid that may have been released while cooling (this liquid has major flavour). Add the remaining 2 tablespoons of butter, brown sugar, cornstarch, lemon juice and salt and stir to combine.

6. Preheat the oven to 425°F. Alternatively, you can cook the galette over the hot coals or on the barbeque for even more smoky flavour. Cooking time will vary depending on your heat source, but I find galettes cook quite quick on the barbeque, usually within 20 minutes, so check regularly. The rest of this recipe will assume oven preparation.

7. Remove the dough from the fridge 10 minutes before you're ready to use it. Line a baking sheet with parchment paper. Lightly flour the working surface and rolling pin and roll the dough into a large 12-inch circle about a 1/4 inch thick. Transfer to the baking sheet.

8. Arrange the peach filling in the centre of the dough leaving a 2-inch boarder around the edge. Fold the edge up and over the peaches. Brush the dough with the beaten egg and sprinkle with turbinado sugar.

9. Bake for 40-45 minutes, or until the crust is golden and the centre is bubbling. Remove and cool before slicing. Sprinkle with a few fresh leaves of basil and serve.

Farm on the 14th

black currants

Though the main focus for Farm on the 14th is their microgreens (see page 122), they also offer black currants during summer months. Black currants are small dark berries with a tart, acidic flavour. They make lovely jams and bring a blissful balance to sweet baked goods.

Black currants grow on a hardy, frost tolerant bush that handles Canadian winters quite well. The bush prefers to grow in areas with lots of sun and air flow. They flower in the early spring and are self-pollinating though they produce higher yields with the help of bees and other pollinators. Fruit harvest is for a few short weeks between July and August and once ripe, they need to be picked quickly before they fall to the ground or get snatched up by birds.

Black Currant and White Chocolate Streusel Muffins

- Makes 12 -

These muffins are a fabulous blend of flavours and textures; bursting with tart, juicy currants followed with a soft, comforting crumb, surprising bites of sweet white chocolate and crowned with a crunchy streusel.

Ingredients

1 1/4 cup (156 g) all-purpose flour

1/2 cup (100 g) brown sugar, lightly packed

2 teaspoons baking powder

1 teaspoon cinnamon

1/4 teaspoon kosher salt

3/4 cup (180 ml) whole milk, at room temperature

2 large eggs, at room temperature

1/3 cup (76 g) unsalted butter, melted

2 teaspoons vanilla extract

1 cup (110 g) fresh black currants

1/2 cup (85 g) white chocolate chips

Streusel Topping

1/4 cup (31 g) all-purpose flour

1/4 cup (50 g) brown sugar, lightly packed

2 tablespoons (25 g) granulated sugar

1/2 teaspoon cinnamon

Pinch kosher salt

1/4 cup (57 g) unsalted butter, melted

Directions

1. Preheat the oven to 375°F. Grease or line a 12-cup muffin tin.
2. **To prepare the muffins**, whisk together the flour, brown sugar, baking powder, cinnamon and salt in a large bowl.
3. In a separate bowl, whisk together the milk, eggs, butter and vanilla. Pour into the dry ingredients and stir until combined and smooth.
4. Gently fold in the black currants and white chocolate chips.
5. Fill 2/3 of each muffin cup with batter.
6. **To prepare the streusel**, combine the flour, brown sugar, granulated sugar, cinnamon and salt in a small bowl. Add the butter and stir until small clumps form. Sprinkle over each muffin.
7. Bake for 20-25 minutes or until a toothpick inserted into the centre of a muffin comes out clean. Let cool for 5 minutes in the tin and then transfer to a wire rack to cool completely before enjoying. Store in an airtight container at room temperature for up to 2 days.

T & S Gignac Farms

watermelon

Ted and Sherry Gignac along with their sons Branden and Brock own and operate T & S Gignac Farms. This family farm grows a variety of crops including strawberry, corn, soybean, rye and has now grown watermelon for nearly 20 years. They began their watermelon operation with 20 acres but have progressively expanded to around 800 acres of watermelon under their new label Sunvine, making them the largest producer of watermelon in Ontario.

Watermelons are heavy feeders meaning they require a lot of nutrients to thrive. The sandy loam soil of Norfolk County in combination with our hot summers offer the nutrient-rich, fertile growing ground they need. The watermelon plant must undergo pollination to produce fruit, which occurs by the male flowers pollinating the female flowers with the help of our bee friends and other pollinator insects.

Depending on the variety of watermelon, it can take between 75 to 90 days from planting to harvest. Watermelons do not increase Brix (sugar) levels once harvested, so it takes knowledge and skill to pick them at just the right time. Branden shared a few ways to identify a ripe watermelon that I am pleased to include here: contrasting light and dark stripes on the rind (depending on variety), a dried up brown tendril (the curled up bit of vine) and a yellow bottom, also known as a ground spot, which indicates that it has spent enough time ripening on the vine. These are good indicators that the watermelon is ready for harvest. Watermelons are available late July until early September.

Watermelon Lemonade

- Serves 4 -

Can you think of anything more refreshing on a hot Summer's day than a tall glass of this Watermelon Lemonade? This drink is sweet and tart with a delicious undertone of colourful watermelon. Enjoy it as is or add a shot of your favourite spirit.

Ingredients

3/4 cup (150 g) granulated sugar

3/4 cup (180 ml) water

1 cup (240 ml) fresh lemon juice, about 6 lemons

6 cups fresh cubed watermelon (around 2 pounds)

Ice

Directions

1. Combine the sugar and water in a small saucepan over medium heat to create a simple syrup. Stir regularly until the sugar has completely dissolved, about 5 minutes, then let cool.

2. Roll the lemons around on your counter to soften. Cut in half and squeeze the juice into a liquid measuring cup until you have 1 cup or 240 ml. Pour through a fine mesh sieve to collect pulp and any seeds.

3. Add the watermelon cubes to a high-speed blender and blend on high for 30 seconds or until smooth. Pour through a fine mesh sieve to collect the pulp.

4. Add the simple syrup, lemon juice and watermelon juice to a large jug. Stir to combine and refrigerate until cold, at least 30 minutes. Serve over ice.

Inasphere Estate Winery

tomatoes

Inasphere is owned and operated by Ryan and Shantel Bosgoed. Ryan is the third generation of his family to farm the special land. They farm a variety of produce including wine grapes, tomatoes, cabbage, squash, and onions. As Inasphere is located on marshland, the proximity of the water allows for this land to harbour some of the most fertile soil in Norfolk County providing the produce with its amazing flavour and magnificent colour.

In addition to an array of seasonal fruit, vegetables and preserves, you will also find San Marzano and field tomatoes at Inasphere's farm market. There's nothing quite like a fresh, ripe field tomato! They are sweet, sour and tangy: the perfect combination and simply delicious on their own with just a sprinkle of salt. Tomato plants require full sun and mineral-rich, well-drained but moisture-retentive soil to thrive. Inasphere boasts the ideal location for thriving tomato plants for several reasons; they have the desired loamy soils of Norfolk County, the surrounding marshland provides moisture and vital nutrients to the plants and the growing fields are completely open offering full sun for several hours a day leading to a greater yield. Staking the tomatoes also aids in a higher yield as it provides more air flow and keeps more insects and pests away in comparison to tomatoes sprawling on the ground.

Tomatoes require 60-100 days to reach harvest depending on the variety. A tomato is ripe when it's firm, vivid in colour and its skin turns from dull to glossy. Tomatoes taste best when they are harvested when ripe, but can also be picked when green as they will continue to ripen off the vine. Picking them when green makes them more resilient to processing and shipping, but some of the flavour and texture is sacrificed in the process; this is why buying fresh and local is best! Tomatoes are available at Inasphere from around mid-July until first frost.

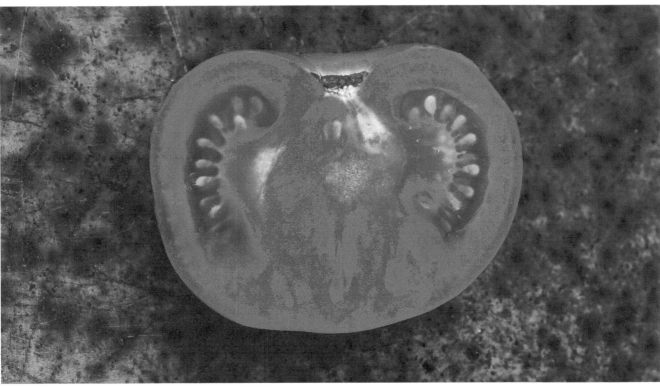

Rustic Tomato Galette with Thyme and Honey

- Serves 8 -

The bounty of succulent tomatoes summer provides deserves to be showcased. A herb speckled savoury pie crust is paired with peak-season tomatoes for a simple yet impressive looking dish. Enjoy as an appetizer or as a light dinner.

Ingredients

Dough

1 1/2 cups (188 g) all-purpose flour

6 sprigs of thyme, leaves only

1/2 teaspoon kosher salt

10 tablespoons (142 g) cold unsalted butter chopped into small cubes

2-3 tablespoons cold water

Filling

2 pounds fresh tomatoes (about 2 large and 2 small tomatoes)

2 tablespoons + 1/2 teaspoon kosher salt

1/2 cup full-fat sour cream

4 sprigs thyme, leaves only, finely chopped

1 garlic clove, minced

1 tablespoon + 1 tablespoon olive oil

1/2 tablespoon lemon zest

1/4 teaspoon ground black pepper

1/2 cup crumbled feta

1 tablespoon + 1 tablespoon honey

Directions

1. **To prepare the dough**, place the flour, thyme leaves, and salt in a food processor and pulse a few times to mix. Add in the cold butter cubes and pulse around 10 times or until the butter is in small clumps. Turn on the food processor and add in the water one tablespoon at a time until the dough comes together and forms a ball.

2. Transfer the dough onto a lightly floured surface. Gently knead for about one minute, shape into a ball and wrap with plastic wrap. Refrigerate for at least one hour.

3. **To prepare the filling**, slice the tomatoes about a 1/4 inch thick. Use the 2 tablespoons of salt to sprinkle on both sides of the tomato slices and set on a baking sheet lined with paper towels. Lay more paper towels on top and gently press down. Let sit for 10 minutes. This step is important because the salt draws out excess water from the tomatoes so you are not left with a soggy galette.

4. In a medium bowl, combine the sour cream, thyme, garlic, 1 tablespoon of olive oil, lemon zest, pepper and remaining 1/2 teaspoon of salt.

5. Preheat the oven to 425°F. Line a baking sheet with parchment paper. Remove the dough from the fridge 10 minutes before you're ready to use it.

6. Lightly flour the working surface and rolling pin and roll the dough into a large 12-inch circle about a 1/4 inch thick. Transfer to the baking sheet. Spread on the filling leaving a 2-inch border around the edge. Layer the tomato slices over top, sprinkle on the feta and drizzle on 1 tablespoon of honey. Brush the sides with the remaining 1 tablespoon of olive oil.

7. Bake for 45-50 minutes or until the edges are golden and the middle is bubbling. Remove from the oven and let cool for 5 minutes before slicing. Drizzle with the remaining 1 tablespoon of honey before serving.

Creamy Pea and Parmesan Dip

- Makes 2 cups -

This light, fresh dip makes a flavourful addition to veggie trays, sandwiches and wraps, or add a spoonful to your favourite pasta sauce for an extra zing.

Ingredients

2 cups peas, fresh or frozen

1/2 cup freshly grated parmesan cheese

1/2 cup plain yogurt

1 garlic clove

2 tablespoons olive oil

1 tablespoon lemon juice

1/2 teaspoon kosher salt

1/4 teaspoon ground black pepper

Directions

1. Bring a medium pot of water to a boil. Blanche the peas for about 1 minute or until they are soft and float to the top. Quickly place in ice water.

2. Drain the peas and put them in a food processor with the rest of the ingredients. Pulse until combined and smooth. I like to pulse until the mixture is cohesive but there are still small chunks for texture, but you can pulse until completely smooth if you prefer. If the dip is too thick, add more olive oil to thin. Store in an airtight container in the refrigerator for up to 1 week.

Raspberry, Cucumber and Rosemary Spritz

- Serves 2 -

Sipping this drink makes me daydream of sitting on a porch swing on a warm night as I take in the magnificent sunset beyond the water's edge. The combination of flavours offer a lovely balance of floral, tangy and sweet. Enjoy it as is or turn it into a tipple with a splash of gin or vodka.

Ingredients

1 small cucumber

8 raspberries

1 sprig rosemary, leaves only

1 teaspoon wildflower honey

Juice of 1 lime

300 ml tonic water

Ice

Garnish

2 lime slices

2 rosemary sprigs

Directions

1. Use a vegetable peeler to ribbon the cucumber, making 6 ribbons in total.

2. Place 4 of the cucumber ribbons and the raspberries, rosemary leaves, honey and lime juice into a large glass or small bowl. Muddle (squish) to combine and release the juices.

3. Gently press the remaining two cucumber ribbons onto the side of your glasses to achieve the same look as the picture, or simply place them into the glasses instead.

4. Strain the juice through a fine mesh sieve and divide it between the two glasses. Add a scoop of ice to each glass and top with the tonic water. Add a lime slice and rosemary sprig to each glass for garnish and serve.

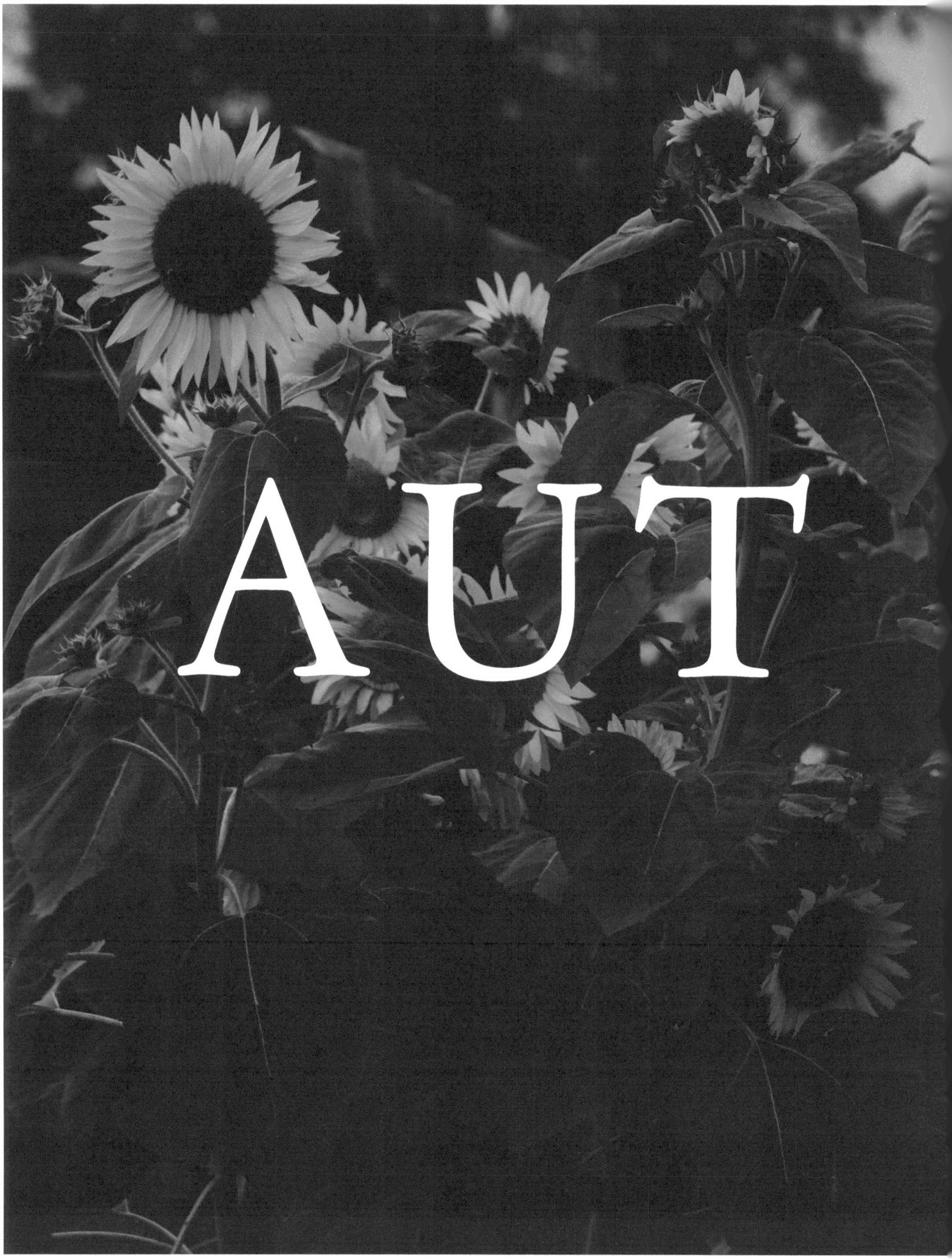
AUT

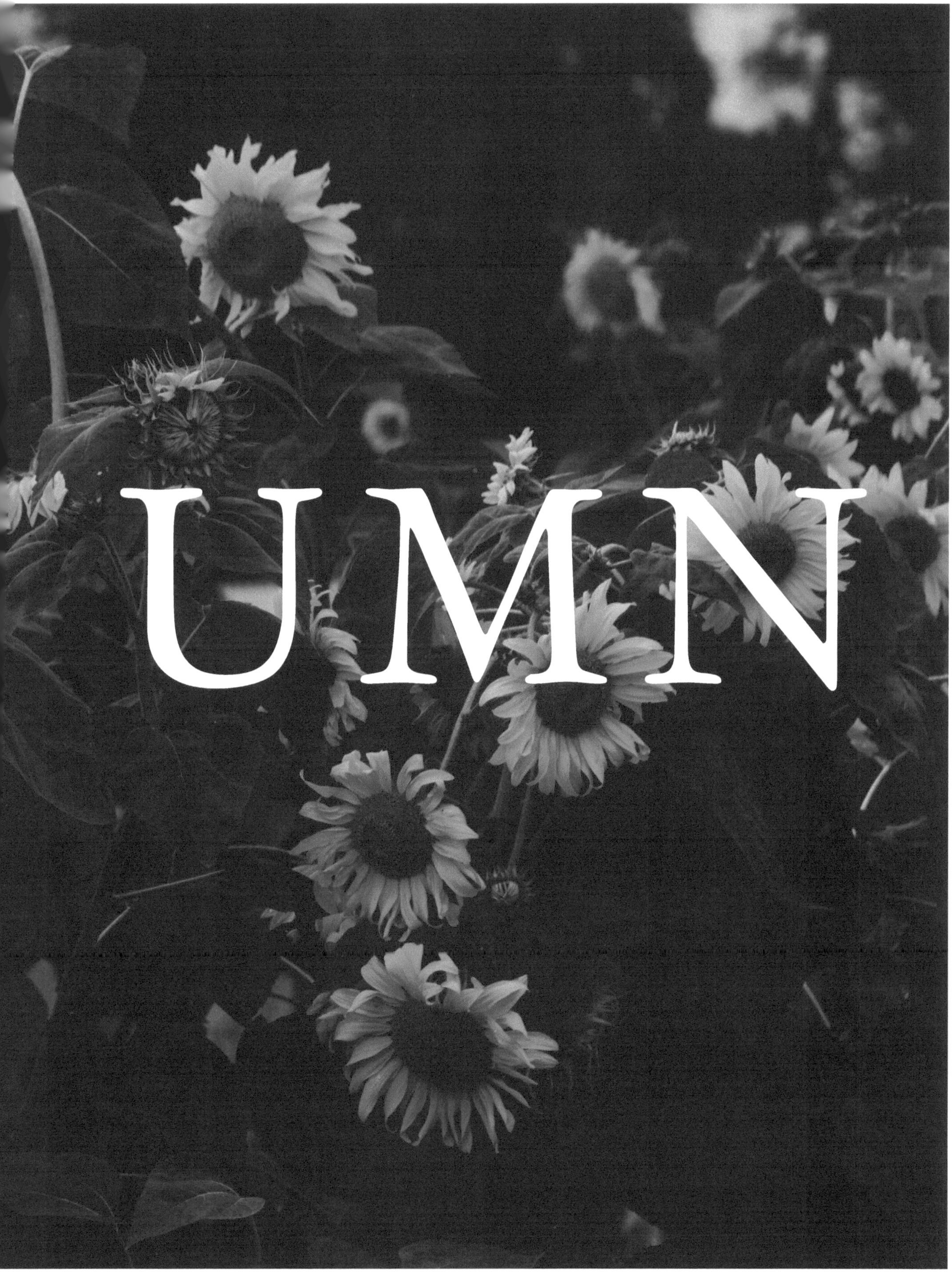
UMN

A U T U M N:

Welcome the cool, refreshing mornings as the sun starts to feel a little more friendly and as the smells turn from new and sprouting to ripe and earthy. Allow the mind, body and soul to take a deep breath; come home to yourself. This season reminds us that our lives go through cycles of bloom, harvest, death and rebirth just as in nature. Acknowledge your growth and thank the earth for your abundant harvest.

Black Creek Bee Co.

honey

Husband and wife duos Tim and Rachel Cromwell and Paul and Kristen Kuchar joined forces to create Black Creek Bee Co., paying homage to the creek that runs through their bee farm as its namesake. The business was started from scratch in 2019 and the team has since faced the many hurdles and learning opportunities that accompany bee farming with elegance.

The 100% pure unpasteurized Ontario honey is prepared and jarred completely by hand in small batches directly on the farm with only the surplus of honey being harvested to ensure the bees remain happy and fed. Honey extraction is a careful and methodical process that requires structure and proficiency when removing the honey frames from the hive. Honeycomb, found within the honey frames, hold the individual cells that honeybees fill with honey and cover with beeswax, known as capping. The capping must be removed in order to extract the honey though even with it removed, heavy force still needs to be used to draw out the honey. A honey extractor is a large barrel drum that vertically holds the honey frames and uses centrifugal force to spin and fling the honey out. The

Kristen Kuchar and Rachel Cromwell

honey collects at the bottom of the drum and it is then strained to remove any bits of bees wax while still maintaining the beneficial pollen and natural enzymes that honey contains. It is then carefully jarred by hand and ready to make its way onto your shelf.

In addition to honey production, the team also uses their social networks to spread awareness of the declining bee population due to things like pesticides, loss of habitat and loss of flower varieties that provide pollen and nectar. Planting pollinator-attracting plants like borage, marigolds and sunflowers among or near crops is essential for the pollination and growing of our food and keeping our hard-working pollinators happy. The many crops of Norfolk County wouldn't be possible without our bee friends!

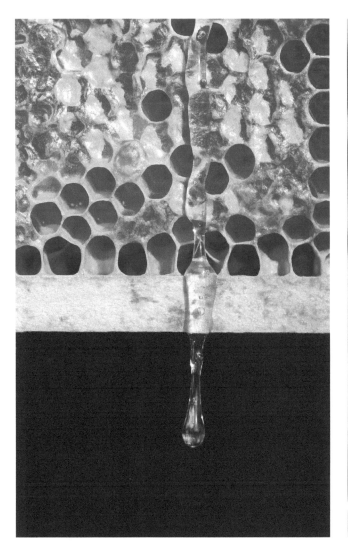

Burnt Honey and Chai Mousse

- Serves 6 -

This honey mousse is light as a feather but full of flavour! Why burnt honey? When cooked, the sugars in the honey oxidize and break down in a process called caramelization. This process turns the honey nutty and fragrant and enhances the flavours already within the honey (think floral, fruity, woody and earthy). The flavour is truly magical, especially when paired with warming chai spices. Enjoy this mousse as is, or layer it into cakes, cupcakes or bars.

Ingredients

1/2 cup (200 g) wildflower honey

3/4 cup (180 ml) + 2 cups (480 ml) whipping cream

1 teaspoon + 1 teaspoon vanilla extract

1/2 teaspoon cinnamon

2 chai tea bags

1 1/2 teaspoons powdered gelatin + 1 1/2 tablespoons cold water

1/4 cup (32 g) icing sugar

Kosher salt

Garnish

Additional wildflower honey

Bee pollen

Directions

1. Add the honey to a medium saucepan over medium heat. The honey will begin to bubble. Continue to heat until the honey starts to turn a dark amber colour, with a nutty aroma, about 5 minutes. Once dark, stir in the 3/4 cup of cream, 1 teaspoon of vanilla, cinnamon and a pinch of salt. Bring to a simmer, stirring to dissolve any honey that may have hardened when the cream was added.

2. Remove from the heat and add in the chai tea bags. Cover and let infuse for at least 30 minutes.

3. In a small bowl, combine the gelatin and cold water. Let sit for 5 minutes to bloom.

4. Remove the tea bags from the liquid ingredients and return to medium heat. Bring to a simmer and stir in the gelatin until dissolved.

5. Strain through a fine mesh sieve into a large bowl and let cool to room temperature.

6. Using a stand mixture fitted with the whisk attachment, whip the remaining 2 cups of cream. As the cream is whipping, slowly add in the icing sugar in two additions, whipping after each one. Add in the remaining 1 teaspoon of vanilla and a pinch of salt and continue to whip until stiff peaks form.

7. Using a spatula, *gently* fold the whipped cream into the cooled liquid ingredients in three additions until smooth and just combined. Do not stir vigorously as this will deflate the whipped cream.

8. Transfer the mousse to your serving dishes and refrigerate for at least 5 hours or overnight. The mousse is set once the texture has stabalized and become slightly more dense. Drizzle with more honey and top with bee pollen before serving. Store covered in the refrigerator for up to 3 days.

Schuyler Farms LTD

apples

Apples, the ultimate symbol of fall. Fresh apples welcome cool crisp air, vivid leaves and cozy sweaters. Schuyler farms grows a variety of apples with varying colours, sizes, crispness, sweetness and flavour. They are a member of the Norfolk Fruit Growers Association which packages, stores and markets their apple crop.

From planting, apple trees take at least 3 years to bear fruit and prefer areas of full sunlight and sandy loam soils with good drainage for root health. There are numerous diseases and insects that can attack an apple, so it requires a great extent of knowledge about crop protection to keep an orchard safe. Crop protection starts from when the first bud breaks until harvest. Maintaining an orchard is no small feat especially as pruning and harvesting are done by hand. Pruning is essential as it maintains the overall health of the tree, provides more circulation and sun exposure throughout the limbs and encourages healthier, larger fruit.

Like all fruit trees, apples must be pollinated to bear fruit. This requires the transfer of pollen from the stamen (male) to the stigma (female) within a blossom. This is done with the help of bees and other pollinating insects or by cross-pollination with pollen from other nearby trees.

Apples are ripe when they are easy to separate from the tree and the seeds inside are brown. With the help of ladders, they are gently harvested by hand and placed into large storage bins in the orchard. The apples are then sent to be graded based on their size, colour and quality. Apple harvest lasts from September into November.

Buckwheat and Spiced Apple Pancakes

- Makes 10 -

I would argue that pancakes are the best breakfast food. They are versatile, fluffy, and bring a little nostalgia with every bite. These buckwheat pancakes probably aren't the pancakes you grew up on, but they make up for their humble appearance with a wonderful nutty flavour and hearty texture. Buckwheat flour is made from the seeds of buckwheat, a flowering crop. It is more nutritionally dense than standard wheat flour and is naturally gluten-free. The earthy flavour of the buckwheat makes a lovely pairing with the sweet, stewed apples. These pancakes are a wholesome way to begin your day.

Ingredients

Stewed Apples

4 medium apples, peeled and chopped into small cubes (Courtland, Granny Smith or Jonagold)

2 tablespoons (28 g) unsalted butter

1/4 cup (55 g) brown sugar

1/2 teaspoon cinnamon

1/4 teaspoon all spice

Pancakes

1 cup (120 g) buckwheat flour

2 tablespoons (26 g) brown sugar

1 teaspoon baking soda

1 teaspoon baking powder

1/2 teaspoon cinnamon

1/2 teaspoon kosher salt

1 cup (240 ml) whole milk, at room temperature

2 tablespoons (28 g) melted unsalted butter, plus more for skillet

2 large eggs, at room temperature

1/2 teaspoon vanilla extract

Directions

1. **To prepare the stewed apples**, melt the butter over medium heat in a large saucepan; add the apples. Cook, stirring regularly, until apples are nearly tender, about 6-7 minutes.

2. Stir in the brown sugar, cinnamon and all spice. Cook for an additional 2-3 minutes, or until tender.

3. **To prepare the pancakes**, combine the buckwheat flour, brown sugar, baking soda, baking powder, cinnamon and salt in a large bowl. In a separate bowl, combine the milk, melted butter, eggs and vanilla. Stir the wet ingredients into the dry ingredients until just combined.

4. Fold 1 cup of the stewed apples into the pancake batter.

5. Heat a lightly buttered skillet or frying pan over medium-high heat. Pour the batter onto the hot skillet, using approximately 1/3 cup for each pancake. Cook for 2-3 minutes, or until small bubbles form on the surface of the pancake. Flip and cook on the opposite side for 1-2 minutes or until golden brown.

6. Gently stir the batter before each pour as buckwheat flour tends to separate. Repeat the process with the remaining batter, brushing the skillet with additional butter as needed. Serve with butter, maple syrup and the additional stewed apples.

Farm on the 14th

Asian Pears

In addition to their black currants and microgreens, Farm on the 14th is also prized for their Asian pears! Asian pears are sweet, tart and aromatic with delicate floral notes. They have a high water content and are noticeably more firm and crunchy in comparison to other pears. They are delicious raw, or in cooking applications like baking, stewing and poaching.

Asian pear trees prefer areas of full sun and rich, well-draining soil and are cold-hardy, requiring chill time over the winter months in order to produce fragrant white blossoms in the spring. The trees are cross-pollinating which means they need to be planted in multiples in order to produce a yield and once planted, it can take three to five years before any fruit is produced. Asian pears are harvested in the early fall and are ripe enough to be picked when they are green-brown, smell sweet and snap easily off the tree.

Spiced Asian Pear Cake with Brown Butter Buttercream

- Serves 10 -

This cake is filled with fresh, juicy pear and the warming spices of fall and finished with a nutty brown butter buttercream. Browning the butter first is key to taking the buttercream from "good" to "glorious." This cake is simple to make, but is sure to impress with its effortless elegance.

Ingredients

Cake

3 cups shredded Asian pears, about 6-8 pears

2 cups (250 g) all-purpose flour

1 1/2 teaspoons baking powder

1/2 teaspoon baking soda

2 teaspoons cinnamon

1/2 teaspoon cardamom

1/4 teaspoon all spice

1/2 teaspoon kosher salt

2 large eggs, at room temperature

3/4 cup (165 g) brown sugar, packed

1/2 cup (100 g) granulated sugar

1 cup (240 ml) milk, at room temperature

1/2 cup (110 ml) vegetable oil

2 teaspoons vanilla extract

Buttercream

1 cup (227 g) unsalted butter

2 1/2 cups (325 g) icing sugar

1 teaspoon vanilla extract

2 tablespoons heavy cream

Pinch of kosher salt

Directions

1. Preheat the oven to 350°F. Butter and flour two 6-inch round cake pans and line the bottoms with parchment paper. After shredding the pears, make sure they are well drained by wrapping them in a kitchen towel or paper towels and pressing out any extra liquid.

2. **To prepare the cake**, whisk together the flour, baking powder, baking soda, cinnamon, cardamom, all spice and salt in a medium bowl.

3. In a separate large bowl, whisk together the eggs, brown sugar and granulated sugar until slightly thickened and light in colour. Then whisk in the milk, oil and vanilla. Add to the dry ingredients and stir until combined. Gently fold in the grated pears.

4. Evenly divide the batter between the prepared pans and smooth out the tops. Bake for 35-40 minutes, or until a toothpick inserted into the centre of the cake comes out clean. Cool the cakes in the pans for 20 minutes, then remove and let cool completely on a wire rack.

5. **To prepare the buttercream**, place the butter in a medium-sized pan over medium heat. Once melted, the butter will begin to foam and sizzle. Occasionally stir to make sure the butter does not burn. After 5-8 minutes, the foam will subside and the butter will turn golden brown and smell nutty and sweet. Remove from the heat and transfer to a bowl. Place the bowl in the freezer for 10-20 minutes or until it has firmed back up to *room temperature* butter.

6. In a stand mixer fitted with the paddle attachment, cream the browned butter on medium-high speed for 2-3 minutes, or until light and fluffy. Lower the speed and gradually add in the icing sugar a 1/2 cup at a time. Once the icing sugar is fully incorporated, add in the vanilla, heavy cream and salt and increase the speed to medium-high. Beat for an additional 2-3 minutes or until light and fluffy.

7. **To assemble the cake**, place one cake layer on a serving plate or cake stand and spread the top with buttercream. Top with the other cake layer and spread the rest of the buttercream across the top and sides of the cake. I put a light layer of buttercream on the sides to create a rustic "naked" look. Slice and serve! Store in an airtight container at room temperature for up to 2 days.

Kernal Peanuts

peanuts

Yes, peanuts grow in Ontario! Kernal Peanuts is owned and operated by Nancy and Ernie Racz on Ernie's family farm. Ernie began experimenting with peanuts when difficulties occurred with the tobacco industry in the late 1970's which had been the family farm's main crop up to that point. By 1982, the couple had established their business and were selling peanuts commercially; they are now the largest grower of peanuts in Canada!

Peanuts are planted from seed and develop into a green, oval-leafed plant about 18 inches tall. The peanut plant flowers above ground, but fruits below ground. The yellow peanut flower will pollinate itself and form a peanut ovary, known as a peg. The peg grows down and away from the plant into the soil where it will take form as a peanut pod. Depending on the variety, each plant will produce at least 20 peanut pods with one to three nuts in each pod. Light sandy soil is ideal for growing peanuts as it allows the peg to penetrate the soil and provides the peanut pods space to grow.

Peanuts are planted at the end of May and are ready for harvest when the leaves begin to yellow near the end of September. The peanuts are then cleaned, dried and graded prior to being sent for roasting or further processing. There are four varieties of peanuts, but Kernal's favourite is the Valencia as it is sweeter and best for roasting. In addition to roasted peanuts, Nancy and Ernie also fill their store front with fresh peanut butter, a variety of confections and their famous peanut butter pie.

Peanut Butter Meringue Clouds

- Makes 16 -

Hello, peanut butter lovers! I know there's many of you. These meringue clouds are salty, sweet and taste just like a peanut butter cookie but with a light, crunchy twist. They take patience and a longer time in the oven than most sweet treats, but they are so worth the wait. You'll understand once you try one! Enjoy them as-is, or pair with your favourite ice cream.

Ingredients

3 large egg whites (90 g), at room temperature

1/4 teaspoon cream of tartar

1/2 cup (100 g) granulated sugar

1/3 cup (80 g) crunchy or smooth peanut butter made from 100% peanuts

1/4 teaspoon vanilla extract

Garnish

Peanut butter

Crushed peanuts

Directions

1. Preheat the oven to 200°F. Line two baking sheets with parchment paper.

2. Add the egg whites to the bowl of a stand mixer fitted with the whisk attachment (you can also use a high-speed hand mixer). Beat at medium-high speed until the egg whites are foamy. Add the cream of tartar and continue to whisk until the egg whites turn creamy white and start to fluff up. At this point, start adding the sugar about one tablespoon at a time while the mixer is still on. Let the sugar fully incorporate before adding more. If needed, stop the mixer and use a spatula to scrape down any sugar granules into the egg whites. Continue to beat on medium-high speed until the whites are thick, glossy and hold stiff peaks when the whisk is lifted out of the bowl. This may take up to 5 minutes.

3. Remove the bowl from the mixer and drizzle over the peanut butter and vanilla. Use a spatula to gently fold the peanut butter into the meringue until streaky, but not fully incorporated.

4. Drop heaping tablespoons of meringue onto the baking sheets, about 2 inches apart. If you would like the meringues to look more uniform, you can use a piping bag and pipe swirls of meringue onto the baking sheets. Bake for 90 minutes, rotating the baking sheets from front to back halfway through (at the 45 minute mark). Turn off the heat and let the meringues cool completely in the oven for at least one hour.

5. Store the meringues in an airtight container for up to two weeks. Top with a drizzle of peanut butter and crushed peanuts before serving.

Ryder Farms

sweet potatoes

In addition to green onions (page 58) and their other main commodities, Ryder Farms are also producers of sweet potatoes. Sweet potatoes are often referred to as "roots" as they are actually a root vegetable and not a potato. Storage roots or vine cuttings (called slips) are planted in late May to early June after the danger of frost has passed. As they are sensitive to the cold, sandy-loam soil is preferred as it warms rapidly and allows roots room to spread, contributing to a successful production.

Sweet potato harvest begins in early September and continues through October. The roots grow on a thick vine and in order to be harvested, the vine must be shredded to expose the rows. After shredding, a modified potato digger is used to go deep into the ground and slowly bring up the roots onto a running belt. As the roots come up, they are graded by size, shape and condition and placed into bins, all of which occur in the field, right on the harvester.

After harvest, the sweet potatoes require immediate curing to promote the healing of any bruises that occurred during harvest, to increase post-harvest life and to promote the conversion of starches to sugars, giving them their notorious sweet flavour. To cure, the potatoes are kept in a well-circulated and high-humidity space for several weeks to months. They can then be distributed or moved into long term storage.

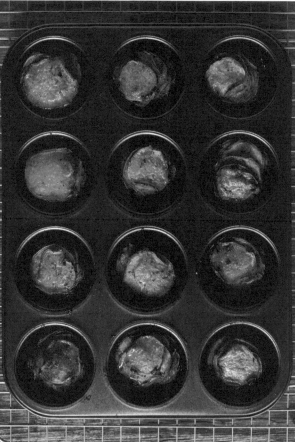

Brown Butter and Thyme Sweet Potato Stacks

- Serves 4-6 -

These sweet potato stacks make the perfect side-dish to any meal. They're fun, flavourful and are sure to be a regular request at your dinner table. The secret to these stacks is thinly slicing the potatoes which, when baked, makes the edges crisp and caramelized with a buttery soft centre.

Ingredients

5 medium sweet potatoes

1/2 cup (113 g) unsalted butter

2 tablespoons chopped fresh thyme, leaves only

1/2 cup freshly grated parmesan cheese

1 teaspoon kosher salt

1 teaspoon ground black pepper

1/2 teaspoon smoked paprika

Directions

1. Preheat the oven to 400°F. Grease a 12-cup muffin tin.

2. Use a mandolin to carefully slice sweet potatoes into 1/8 inch-thick slices. A sharp knife can be used instead but using a mandolin will be much easier and quicker. Place the slices in a large bowl.

3. To brown the butter, place the butter in a medium-sized pan over medium heat. Once melted, the butter will begin to foam and sizzle. Occasionally stir to make sure the butter does not burn. After 5-8 minutes, the foam will subside and the butter will turn golden brown and smell nutty and sweet. At this point, remove the pan from the heat and carefully pour the butter over the sweet potato slices.

4. Add the rest of the ingredients to the bowl and toss to evenly coat.

5. Layer the sweet potato slices evenly in the prepared muffin tin stacking the layers all the way to the top.

6. Cover with foil and roast for 30 minutes. Remove the foil and roast for another 20-25 minutes or until the potatoes are tender in the middle and golden brown around the edges. Use a knife to run along the edges of the potatoes to loosen them from the tin and serve.

Inasphere Estate Winery

wine

Norfolk County's proximity to The Great Lakes provides a continental climate, suitable for many grape varieties. The sandy soils provide excellent drainage and force the grape vines to grow deeper into the earth for moisture. The length of growing season and date of harvest varies greatly depending on the temperature and grape variety.

Ryan and Shantel planted their first crop of grapes in 2008 and have been diversifying and introducing new varieties to add to the flavour of their wines ever since. They are proud to share that the entire wine production is done on site: the growing, harvesting, fermentation, pressing and finally the bottling of the wine. Ryan and Shantel encourage their guests to immerse themselves in the place where their wine was created by relaxing on the patio and taking in the stunning view of the biosphere below, while enjoying a glass of wine.

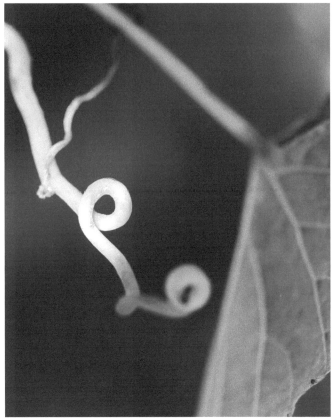

Red Wine Brownies

- Makes 12 -

There is something so decadent about the combination of red wine and chocolate. The dark chocolate in these brownies pairs perfectly with the fragrant notes of dark fruit, vanilla and cedar in the Inasphere Cabernet Sauvignon. Let yourself indulge in every bite of this rich and fudgy boozy brownie.

Ingredients

- 1/2 cup (113 g) unsalted butter
- 3/4 cup (112 g) chopped dark chocolate
- 1/2 cup (100 g) brown sugar, lightly packed
- 1/2 cup (100 g) granulated sugar
- 2 large eggs, at room temperature
- 1/2 cup (120 ml) red wine (Inasphere 2019 Cabernet Sauvignon)
- 3/4 cup (94 g) all-purpose flour
- 1/2 cup (55 g) cocoa powder, sifted
- 1 teaspoon vanilla extract
- 1/2 teaspoon kosher salt
- 1/2 cup (85 g) semi-sweet chocolate chips or chunks (optional)

Directions

1. Preheat the oven to 350 °F. Line an 8 x 8-inch pan with parchment paper.
2. In a small saucepan over low heat, melt the butter and dark chocolate, stirring regularly until smooth and there are no clumps.
3. Add the brown sugar and granulated sugar to the bowl of a stand mixer fitted with the whisk attachment. Turn the mixer to medium speed and slowly pour in the melted butter and chocolate. With the mixer still running, add in the eggs one at a time. Beat until the colour of the batter slightly lightens, about 30 seconds.
4. Turn the mixer to low and add in the wine, flour, cocoa powder, vanilla and salt and continue to beat on low until the just combined, about 30 seconds. Fold in the chocolate chips.
5. Pour the batter into the prepared pan and bake for 35-40 minutes, or until a toothpick inserted in the centre of the brownies comes out mostly clean.
6. Allow the brownies to cool in the pan for at least 20 minutes, then remove to cool completely on a wire rack. Slice and serve! Store in an airtight container at room temperature for up to 3 days.

Quick Carrot and Beet Salad

- Serves 4 -

This salad truly is quick and easy to make. It's nothing fancy, rather a simple way to appreciate the fresh, earthy flavours of carrots and beets. I make this salad often, all year round. I will usually make a big batch at the beginning of the week and eat it as part of a snack or as a side to a meal. Enjoy it as is or try it with crumbled feta, fresh chopped dill or toasted walnut pieces (or all three)!

Ingredients

2 large carrots, peeled

1 large beet, peeled

2 tablespoons olive oil

1 1/2 tablespoons apple cider vinegar

3/4 teaspoon kosher salt

Directions

1. There are different ways to create this salad, but I like to use a vegetable peeler by holding on to the top of the carrot and running the peeler down lengthwise to create ribbons. I repeat the same process with the beet, but continually turn the beet to create smaller beet pieces. Alternatively, you can grate the carrots and beet.

2. Add the prepared carrots and beet to a medium bowl and add in the rest of the ingredients and thoroughly mix. Store in an airtight container in the refrigerator for up to 1 week.

WINTER:

Winter's softness and long nights welcome time of reflection, rest and simplicity. It's a season of endings, but hopeful beginnings; a reminder that we must rest and renew in order to rise.

Take time to reconnect with your creativity and find the beauty this season can also hold: the crisp refreshing air, the sparkle of a fresh snowfall, the passionate winds creating songs throughout the pines.

Find warmth around a fireplace, from hearty sustenance, a treasured gathering or from the bone-chilling breeze reminding us of all the warmth we hold within ourselves.

Farm on the 14th

microgreens

Farm on the 14th is owned and operated by Kyle Woolley and partner Laura. After becoming frustrated with the quality and lack of fresh greens during the winter months, they decided to grow their own! All of the greens are hand planted, carefully cared for, hand-cut and packaged individually.

Microgreens are the young greens of vegetables and herbs. Farm on the 14th grows a variety of microgreen types including broccoli, kale, cabbage, mustard, pea, buckwheat and dill. It takes just under two weeks from seed until they are ready to eat. Despite their small size, these aromatic greens pack a nutritional punch, are rich in flavour and bring a splash of colour to any dish. Try them in sandwiches, wraps, soups, omelettes, smoothies, and more!

Kyle and Laura

Falafel-Inspired Microgreen Chickpea Patties

- Makes 12 small patties -

Falafel elicits many funny memories for me as it was my go-to snack after the bar during my university days. Nothing tasted better than a fried falafel on pita at two in the morning. Though the bar scene isn't my thing anymore, I'm still a huge fan of falafel! These falafel-inspired chickpea patties are probably a better decision in comparison as they are filled with nutrient-dense microgreens and are oven-baked rather than fried. They are golden brown and crispy on the outside with a tender, herbaceous centre. Enjoy them as filling for wraps, topping for salads or as a delicious addition to main course. I like them with pita, cucumber slices, tatziki and additional micro greens.

Ingredients

- 1 can (540 ml) unsalted chickpeas, drained, rinsed and patted dry

- 2 packed cups microgreens of choice (I like a blend of pea, dill and cabbage)

- 1/2 cup chopped white onion

- 4-6 garlic cloves, depending on flavour preference

- 1/3 cup chickpea flour, or flour of choice

- 1 tablespoon lemon juice

- 1 tablespoon olive oil, plus more for baking sheet

- 1 teaspoon cumin

- 3/4 teaspoon baking powder

- 3/4 teaspoon kosher salt

- 1/2 teaspoon ground black pepper

- 1/2 teaspoon ground cardamom

- 1/4 teaspoon cayenne pepper (optional)

Directions

1. Add the chickpeas, microgreens and onion to a food processor and pulse to lightly combine. Add the remaining ingredients and pulse until the the mixture resembles a coarse bread crumb texture. If needed, stop partway through and scrape down the sides of the bowl.

2. Transfer to a bowl and let cool in the fridge for at least one hour, or until chilled through. You can also make the dough the day before and let chill overnight.

3. Preheat the oven to 375°F. Line a baking sheet with parchment paper and drizzle it with oil.

4. Measure about two tablespoons of dough and roll into a ball. Place on the baking sheet, roll all sides in the olive oil and then gently push to flatten into a patty about a 1/2 inch thick. Repeat with the remaining dough.

5. Bake for 20 minutes, flip, and cook for an additional 10-15 minutes or until golden brown on both sides.

6. Serve immediately with your choice of accompaniments.

Freezer Friendly. Freeze in a sealed container for up to 3 months. Reheat in the oven at 400°F for 25 minutes or until heated through.

BirdHouse Farm

grass-fed beef

The husband and wife duo, Lauren and Marsha of BirdHouse Farm are leading examples of farming sustainably. They raise 100% grass-fed beef and pasture-raised pork and chicken without the use of any GMO or soy. Marsha's family roots are in agriculture with this passion continuing as she went on to study Agricultural Business at University of Guelph. During her last year of study, she set a goal to raise 100% grass-fed beef and after countless hours of research and preparation, Marsha's first herd of Lowline Angus arrived in March of 2019. The following year, Marsha and Lauren met and they have since continued to expand the farm, implement new sustainability measures and welcome their first child, Hannah.

Marsha, Lauren and baby Hannah

Lauren has no previous farming experience but brings many beneficial skills from his background in engineering. An example of this is the apparatus he designed and built as seen on page 128. This apparatus allows him to easily load and unroll hay bales using their quad. It makes feeding time efficient and keeps the cows happy and fed.

The name of their farm pays homage to the many birdhouses allocated around the pasture (as seen in the top right image on the next page). These birdhouses are essential to naturally sustaining a healthy pasture as they attract beneficial tree swallows which hold a strong relationship with the cows. Flies that are attracted to manure can be extremely bothersome to cows and pose sanitary concerns. Luckily the flies make the perfect meal for hungry swallows!

Most farms try to manage the flies with specialized minerals containing chemicals that are fed to the cows which then ends up in the cow manure and stops the fly eggs from hatching. Unfortunately these chemicals are destructive to the natural ecosystem of a pasture and kill much more than the fly eggs. For example, the chemicals also kill dung beetles which are a necessity to a healthy pasture. Just like flies, dung beetles love manure and use it to sustain their life. The beetles bury the manure into the ground and lay their eggs which helps naturally fertilize and aerate the earth. This builds the soil and replenishes nutrients to the grass being fed to the animals. As you can see from this example, a healthy pasture leads to healthy animals and vice versa creating a beautiful, symbiotic cycle.

This is just a small snippet of the sustainable movements Lauren and Marsha are taking. They continue to research new ways to recycle, reincorporate and redistribute nutrients in the soil to support an ecosystem for many plant and animal species to thrive. They are motivated by their motto "healthy animal = healthy you." The less you interfere with nature and animals' natural behaviours, the healthier the environment, the animals and you will be.

Grass-Fed Beef Meatballs with Feta

- Makes 12-14 meatballs -

These meatballs are a regular in my kitchen because they are quick and easy to make and turn out juicy and flavourful every time. Their versatility is endless as they can be enjoyed as a main dish, on top of spaghetti or as an appetizer.

Ingredients

1 pound grass-fed ground beef

1/3 cup finely chopped white onion

1/3 cup crumbled feta cheese

1/4 cup full-fat sour cream or plain yogurt

2 garlic cloves, minced

1 egg, beaten

1 teaspoon soy sauce

1 teaspoon kosher salt

1/2 teaspoon ground black pepper

1/4 teaspoon cayenne pepper hot sauce (optional)

Directions

1. Preheat the oven to 400°F and line a baking sheet with parchment paper.

2. Add all of the ingredients to a large bowl and mix until thoroughly combined.

3. Use hands to form and roll balls around 1 1/2 inches in size and place onto the prepared baking sheet.

4. Bake 15-20 minutes or until browned and cooked through. Store in an airtight container in the refrigerator for up to 2 days.

Woolley's Lamb

lamb

After completing her studies in Animal Sciences, Carrie Woolley of Woolley's Lamb returned home to Norfolk County to pursue her passion for farming through dedicating her energy to sustainable farming practices. The lamb are raised outside, foraging on cover crops and wooded pastures and grazing through the apple and cherry orchards of Schuyler Farms. Lamb are innocuous and friendly to trees and tree bark in comparison to other ruminant animals. They will graze on fruit that is leftover from harvest and turn it into quickly-composting organic fertilizer. On warm days, the lamb will seek shade under the trees so manure will naturally end up concentrating over the roots of the trees which increases soil and overall orchard health. Lamb are also excellent lawn mowers and keep weeds down which is beneficial as it reduces maintenance costs and reduces soil compaction as heavy machinery is not needed for mowing. These sustainable farming practices result in improved soil-health, offer natural shade and shelter for the animals, reduce feed costs and result in grass-fed lamb that are raised on a 100% pasture diet.

Lamb Chili with Chickpeas and Kale

- Serves 4 -

Chili is one of my favourite cozy Sunday meals, especially on a frigid Winter's day. It's a comforting and hearty dish filled with ingredients I usually have on hand. This chili features ground lamb and chickpeas rather than the typical ground beef and kidney beans and hides a very special ingredient: cocoa powder! I promise you that your chili won't end up tasting like a bowl of chocolate, rather the cocoa powder adds a secret layer of depth and richness to each bite.

Ingredients

2 tablespoons olive oil

1 cup finely diced white onion

1 pound ground lamb

2-3 garlic cloves, minced

1 tablespoon chili powder

1 tablespoon brown sugar

2 teaspoons cumin

2 teaspoons dried oregano

1/2 teaspoon cinnamon

1/2 teaspoon ground black pepper

1 can (796 ml) diced tomatoes

1 large carrot, peeled and diced (about 1 cup)

2 packed cups chopped kale

1 can (540 ml) chickpeas, drained and rinsed

2 cups lamb, beef or vegetable stock

1 tablespoon cocoa powder

Kosher salt

Garnish

Sour cream or plain yogurt

Chopped cilantro

Pickled jalapeños

Directions

1. Heat the oil in a large stockpot over medium-high heat. Add the onions and sauté until soft, about 5 minutes. Push the onions to the sides of the pan and add the lamb. Break apart the lamb as it cooks until browned and cooked through, about 5 minutes. Drain out any excess fat released.

2. Add the garlic, chili powder, brown sugar, cumin, oregano, cinnamon and pepper. Cook for 1 minute or until fragrant. Pour in the tomatoes, scrapping up any brown bits on the bottom of the pan.

3. Stir in the carrot, kale and chickpeas. Cover with the stock, bring to a boil, stir and then turn the heat down to low and simmer for 20-25 minutes or until the carrots are tender and the liquid has reduced and thickened.

4. Remove from the heat, stir in the cocoa powder and add salt to your liking. The amount of salt needed will be dependent on the canned tomatoes and stock you use. Add to serving bowls and top with the sour cream, chopped cilantro and pickled jalapeños. Store in an airtight container in the refrigerator for up to 3 days, or in the freezer for up to 1 month.

Thrive Norfolk

maple syrup

Though Thrive Norfolk is not a farm in the commercial sense, it deserves space in this book as it encapsulates the spirit of Norfolk County and the true meaning of farm-to-table through a 6-course dining experience. Chef Matt celebrates the fresh, seasonal abundance found in Norfolk County by harvesting, preparing and cooking ingredients in their prime. He solely uses ingredients grown on his family farm, or from other local farms within Norfolk County, showcasing them in the "dining room" located in the heart of the Thrive garden.

Although the outdoor dining experience only runs from June to October, the Thrive farm is an all-year affair with seed sowing, transplanting, harvesting, preserving, and soil health maintenance. Come February, Matt and his brother Nick team up to prepare Canada's liquid gold: maple syrup. They hand tap each tree, collect the sap from each bucket daily and spend countless hours tending to the production as the maple sap reduces into syrup (please see pages 138 and 139 for images of maple syrup production).

Every spring, maple trees bloom with tiny flowers in shades of greens, reds and yellows depending on the species. These flowers are an important source of pollen for bees waking up from hibernation and after pollination occurs, the flowers can set seed. The seeds fuse together in twos and form winged samara, better known as the "helicopter" seeds that fall slowly from the tree branches; but these wings are not for aesthetics. As mature maple trees have wide canopies which create a lot of shade below, they developed winged samaras to fly their seeds into sunnier and more hospitable places. This seed spreading system brings glee to those collecting sap as many trees are needed to yield a generous supply. Sap cannot be extracted until the tree is at least 30 years old and it takes over 40 litres of sap to produce just one litre of syrup.

Generally sap starts to flow between mid-February and mid-March depending on the weather conditions. Sap flows best when the daytime temperatures rise above freezing and the nighttime temperatures fall below freezing. These temperature changes create pressure in the trees which causes the sap to flow. Provided ideal temperatures, the sap will continue to flow for about a month.

Tapping starts by drilling a small hole into a healthy, mature tree. A spile (similar to a spout) is inserted into the hole which allows the sap to flow into a collection bucket. When done correctly, this process does not harm the tree. The sap is collected daily and kept in large storage containers until there's enough for boiling. The sap is then transferred to an evaporator which is where the magic happens. The large stainless vat heats the maple sap for many hours which causes evaporation and a series of reactions to occur. A device called a refractometer is used to determine when the syrup is ready and at the right Brix (sugar) content. The syrup is then filtered for sediment and bottled. The syrup Matt and Nick produce is used throughout the Thrive season and into winter in-home caterings.

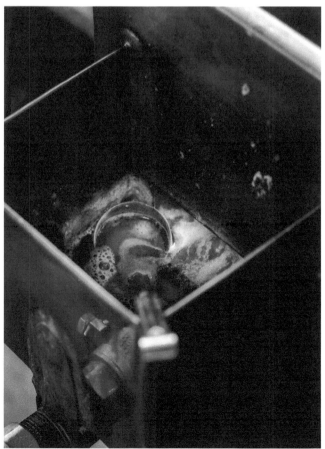

Maple Tuile Cookies

- Makes 10 cookies -

Maple syrup is without a doubt my favourite sweetener! I love using it in anything you use granulated sugar for including cakes, cookies, ice cream and even in coffee. It's boldly sweet and smoky and made right here in Norfolk County!

These maple tuile cookies have become an absolute favourite recipe of mine. I have probably made them too many times... although, I don't think that is possible. Tuiles (pronounced "tweels") are thin, delicate cookies with a distinctive crunch before they dissolve in your mouth. My favourite way to enjoy them is alongside a hot coffee (with maple syrup added of course) but they also make an impressive topping on ice cream, cakes and dessert trays.

Ingredients

1/3 cup (113 g) maple syrup

3 tablespoons (43 g) unsalted butter

1/2 teaspoon vanilla extract

1/3 cup (43 g) all-purpose flour, sifted

Pinch of kosher salt

Directions

1. Preheat the oven to 350°F. Line a baking sheet with parchment paper.

2. Add the maple syrup, butter and vanilla to a small saucepan over medium heat. Allow the butter to melt and then bring to a rapid boil for about 30 seconds.

3. Remove from the heat and whisk in the flour and salt until the mixture is smooth with no lumps. The batter will be slightly runny.

4. Spoon about 1 tablespoon of batter for each cookie onto the baking sheet. Leave about 2-3 inches between each cookie as they will spread while baking. Bake for 10-12 minutes or until the cookies are a dark caramel colour and take on a lace-like appearance.

5. Let cool on the baking sheet for 2 minutes and then transfer to a wire rack to cool completely. They will harden up and develop a delicious crunch as they cool. Store in an airtight container at room temperature for up to 3 days.

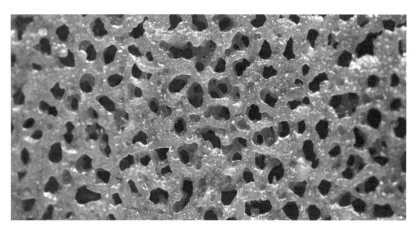

Harissa Roasted Hasselback Squash

- Serves 6 -

This is the kind of dish that I stand over, fork in hand, straight from the oven. Every bite is a lovely combination of savoury, sweet, crunchy and spicy. Roasting the squash makes it sweet and caramelized, while the Hasselback cut makes it beautiful. It's a delicious and unique addition to your table!

If you're unfamiliar with harissa, it is a spicy, smoky, sweet and earthy spice blend native to North Africa. It's often made with caraway, coriander and cumin seeds, peppercorns, garlic and dried chiles. It is fairly easy to find and I have spotted it in many stores across Norfolk County. If spicy isn't your thing, you can substitute the harissa with your favourite dried herb blend and a little smoked paprika.

Ingredients

1 medium butternut squash

Squash Rub

1 tablespoon dried harissa spice

2 tablespoons olive oil

1 tablespoon honey

1 teaspoon minced garlic

Base

1 can (796 ml) diced tomatoes

2 teaspoons dried harissa spice

1 tablespoon minced garlic

1 tablespoon olive oil

1/4 teaspoon kosher salt

Squash Seeds

Seeds from squash

1 teaspoon olive oil

1 teaspoon honey

1/4 teaspoon smoked paprika

1/8 teaspoon nutmeg

Pinch kosher salt

Garnish

Microgreens of choice

Crumbled feta cheese

Pomegranate arils

Lemon zest

Directions

1. Preheat the oven to 400°F.

2. **To prepare the squash**, peel it, cut it in half lengthwise and remove the pulp and seeds. Remove the seeds from the pulp, rinse with warm water and pat dry.

3. Place wooden spoons on either side of the squash halves. This will allow you to slice the squash without slicing all the way through. Make slices in the squash, about 1/4 inch apart.

4. Combine all of the **squash rub** ingredients together in a small bowl. Spoon over the squash and rub until fully covered.

5. Add all of the **base** ingredients to a large dutch oven or roasting dish and mix to combine. Place squash centre down into the base ingredients. Cover with a lid or foil and bake for 30 minutes. Remove the lid and bake for an additional 30-35 minutes or until fork tender.

6. **Prepare the seeds** while the squash is baking. Combine all of the ingredients, minus the seeds, in a small frying pan and heat over medium heat. Once hot, add the seeds and stir constantly until the liquid has reduced and the seeds are golden.

7. Top the squash with the toasted seeds, microgreens, feta cheese, pomegranate arils and lemon zest and serve. Store in an airtight container in the refrigerator for up to 3 days.

Gratitude

Migrant agricultural workers are essential in the farming productions of Norfolk County. As discussed throughout this book, fruit and vegetable farming is very labour-intensive and requires attentive care when planting, harvesting and packaging. Many of these jobs require great skill and expertise in order to be done correctly and to produce a fruitful yield. Many farmers cannot find enough local or domestic employees to work on their farms and rely on the skilled workers who travel from far and wide including the Caribbean, Jamaica, Mexico and Trinidad under the Seasonal Agricultural Worker Program or the Temporary Foreign Worker program.

They bring a variety of experience and knowledge and without them we would struggle to farm at the standard and volume we do. They sacrifice a lot to come to Canada with many working to improve the welfare of their families back home. Some have been returning to the same farm for upwards of 30 years creating a family among the farm and forming a strong connection to the land.

A BIG THANK YOU to the many valuable workers who come here each year to help grow the delicious bounty of Norfolk County!

Gratitude

Thank you to the Demarest family and my family for being honest (and very willing) taste tasters.

Thank you to my partner Matt for supporting this dream of mine and for making sure I got (some) sleep while creating this book.

Thank you to my editor Julia for gracing me with your beautiful energy and bringing clarity to my writing.

Thank you to my mom for being my biggest cheerleader.

Thank you to each and every person along the way who offered resources, direction, tips and insight. This book wouldn't have been possible without you.

And of course, thank you to the many hardworking farmers of Norfolk County who devote their life to bringing us fresh, quality food.

This book was created by all of us!

Glossary

Annuals: Annuals are short-lived plants that germinate, flower, seed and die all within one season.

Horticultural Crops: Horticultural crops include a wide variety of plants including fruits and vegetables to diversify human diets as well as aromatic and ornamental plants to enhance living environments.

Perennials: Perennials are plants that are planted once but continue to survive or grow back every year, for at least three years. Perennials can include some types of flowers, vegetables, fruits, trees, shrubs and grasses.

Sandy Loam Soil: Sandy loam soil is a combination soil type which is predominantly sand with a mixture of silt and clay. This soil type is fertile, acidic, easy to work with and provides good drainage. This soil type favours horticultural crops and just so happens to be the main soil type found within Norfolk County.

Soil pH: Soil pH is a measure of the acidity or alkalinity of a soil. The pH scale runs from 0 to 14, with 7 being neutral. Soils with a pH level of less than 7 are labelled as acidic, while soils with a pH above 7 are labelled as alkaline.

Works Cited

Chapman, L. J. And Putnam, D. F. The Physiography of Southern Ontario. 2nd ed., University of Toronto Press, 1966, 251-255.

Long Point, ON. Directed by Zach Melnick, Striking Balance Inc., 2016. TVO, https://www.tvo.org/video/documentaries/long-point.

CPSIA information can be obtained
at www.ICGtesting.com
Printed in the USA
BVHW012321070323
659915BV00001B/2